Table For Two

THE COOKBOOK FOR COUPLES

*TO ROB AND DANELLE-
BEST WISHES AND
BON APPETIT!*

Table For Two

THE COOKBOOK FOR COUPLES

WARREN CATERSON

 Winfield & Scott Press

Most Winfield & Scott Press books are available at special quantity discounts for bulk purchasers for sales promotions, premiums, fundraising, and educational needs. Special books, book excerpts, or promotional materials can also be created to fit specific needs. For more information please e-mail us at sales@WinfieldAndScottPress.com.

Winfield & Scott Press
1497 Main Street, Suite 185
Dunedin, FL 34698
www.WinfieldAndScottPress.com

Library of Congress Cataloging-in-Publication Data

Caterson, Warren.
        Table for two : the cookbook for couples / Warren
     Caterson.
        p. cm.
        Includes index.
        LCCN 2008906955
        ISBN-13: 978-0-9801568-4-3
        ISBN-10: 0-9801568-4-X

        1. Cookery for two.   I. Title.

     TX652.C38 2009   641.5'612
                                 QBI08-600229

Cover Design: Rebecca Anne Russo
Author Photograph: Darice Michelle Photography
Interior Design: Principle Creative, Jacksonville, Florida

Printed in the United States of America

DEDICATION

~

To my lover and wife, Sherry.

She had the courage to turn her kitchen over to me 26 years ago.

And hopefully she hasn't regretted it since.

Table of Contents

Preface

A leading on-line bookseller lists over 18,000 cookbooks for sale.

18,000! And here's yet another one?

Why?

Simple.

There are many excellent cookbooks on the market today. I own shelves of them. However, this one is different.

How?

In my role as a nonprofit development director and later as a freelance writer, I traveled around the country meeting and speaking with couples, married and unmarried, young and old. Since we often met over a well-prepared meal, the conversation would invariably turn to cooking. We often talked about our most memorable meals, favorite restaurants, or coveted recipes, and time after time I heard this lament: "I'd love to cook more, but I don't know how to cook for only two people."

I heard this from single men and women who knew that eating out on a regular basis was expensive and unhealthy. They wanted to learn to prepare meals that used readily available ingredients and were simple to prepare, but didn't know where to turn.

I heard this from newlyweds who wanted to cook, but couldn't because their parents didn't teach them. Furthermore, when they began buying cookbooks they were frustrated to find that most recipes served a minimum of 4, with many serving 5 to 8. They couldn't do the math to make the recipes smaller.

I heard this from empty nesters that were used to cooking for an entire family, but now needed to learn to cook for two.

As someone who can identify with all of these people, once as a single man, then a family man, and now a soon-to-be empty nester) I'm able to share in their frustration.

I began cooking more than 25 years ago when I was doing inner-city youth work. As I came home each day I retired to the kitchen to spend the next hour or so cooking for my family. It was a relaxing time for me. I'd pour a glass of wine, chop some onions, mince some garlic, and somehow, I was transported to another land. Could I have saved time by defrosting a pre-packaged dinner or nuking an all-in-one meal from some food conglomerate in the mid-west?

Of course.

Did I want to?

Nope.

It may have taken me an hour or more to prepare a meal from scratch, but this was a labor of love. My children grew up strong and healthy. They developed an appreciation for a variety of cultures; we often discussed the origins of the meals as we prepared them together. Everyday around suppertime our home was filled with inviting and delicious aromas such as sautéed onions and garlic, blackened fish, jasmine rice, or steamed green beans. Would I trade all of that for a few minutes of convenience? Not on your life. I think we all yearn for at least one time of the day when we can pour ourselves into a work of love that not only nourishes those that are close to us, but also provides a wonderful opportunity for conversation and interaction. The principles learned from those early days have been with me ever since. Whether cooking for my family, grilling for friends, or catering for a hundred, the love and attention that I put into the meal preparation reminds me that good food and good relationships are gifts that I must cherish.

Perhaps this book, and the ones that follow, will meet the need of all of us who desire to cook but haven't located easy-to-follow recipes for two.

So here's to all the couples and the joy they will find in a lovingly prepared, and shared, meal.

Bon appetit!

MEASURMENTS

Liquid Measure Volume Equivalents

1 teaspoon	= 1/3 tablespoon
1 tablespoon	= 3 teaspoons
2 tablespoons	= 1 fluid ounce
4 tablespoons	= 1/4 cup or 2 ounces
5 1/3 tablespoons	= 1/3 cup or 2 2/3 ounces
8 tablespoons	= 1/2 cup or 1 teacup or 4 ounces
16 tablespoons	= 1 cup or 8-ounces
1/4 cup	= 4 tablespoons
3/8 cup	= 1/4 cup + 2 tablespoons
5/8 cup	= 1/2 cup + 2 tablespoons
7/8 cup	= 3/4 cup + 2 tablespoons
1 cup	= 1/2 pint or 8 fluid ounces
2 cups	= 1 pint or 16 fluid ounces
1 pint	= 2 cups or 16 fluid ounces
1 quart	= 2 pints or 4 cups
1 gallon	= 4 quarts

Table for Two

Cooking Terms

# COOKING TERMS

Note: For an expanded list of cooking terms and ingredients, as well as cooking equipment recommendations, please see my book, Table for Two - The Kitchen Companion, available on-line at TableForTwoCookbooks.com

BLANCHING OR PARBOILING

A technique to partially cook a food in boiling water in preparation for later completion in a dish. Blanching will also loosen the skin of vegetables and will set their color, particularly if the item is immediately plunged into a bowl of ice water. When using this technique, begin your timing the moment the food hits the water. Do not wait for the water to return to a boil.

BRAISING

An ideal method of cooking larger chunks of meat or vegetables that require some tenderizing. Simply brown the meat in a little butter or olive oil then add a little bit of broth or water to the pan and simmer over low heat. This is also an excellent way to cook chicken or fish to keep them from drying out.

BROWNING MEAT

Browning meat in a bit of oil over high heat will not only give it an appealing brown or bronze appearance, it will provide a deeply rich flavor as well. You may have to brown cubed meat in batches to ensure that they brown. Overcrowding the pan will lower the heat and will result in the meat being steamed, rather than browned. Some cookbooks suggest that you dredge the meat in flour before browning. I avoid this because it's the flour that gets browned and not the meat. After all, the purpose of this technique is to brown the natural sugars in the meat and a coating of flour will prevent that from happening.

DEGLAZING

After your meat or vegetable has been browned, you should pour a little wine, stock or water into the pan over high heat and scrape up the rich brown bits that remain. Add this to your soup, stew or sauce for extra flavor.

DREDGING

Thin meats and fish are rolled or tossed in flour or breadcrumbs, which are often seasoned with salt and pepper, before frying or sautéing.

JULIENNE OR MATCHSTICK CUT

Simply cut your vegetable into thin slices, stack the slices then cut them into thin sticks. The sticks may then be cut to your desired length.

MARINATING

This is a technique whereby meats or vegetables are soaked in a flavoring liquid for added pizzazz. However, contrary to popular belief, marinades do little to tenderize tough and inexpensive cuts of meat. The only remedy for that is braising or stewing.

PINCH OR DASH

Start with less than an 1/8 teaspoon and season to taste.

POACHING

A method that gently cooks fish, meat or eggs in stock or water at just below a simmer. This will give the food a delicate and balanced flavor.

REDUCING

Boil a liquid over medium-high or high heat until it is reduced in volume and becomes concentrated.

ROUX

This is a term that describes equal parts of fat and flour which are used to thicken sauces and gravies. For a white roux, the mixture will need to be whisked for at least 4 or 5 minutes; less than that and the sauce will have an off taste. For a brown roux, the mixture will have to be cooked longer, up to an hour, depending on the flavor desired. The longer a roux cooks, the nuttier the flavor.

SAUTÉING

You'll see this term used a lot in this book. It's derived from the French word meaning 'to jump' and is a technique used to cook food quickly with a minimum amount of fat. It's important that you use a heavy skillet that can hold the food in one layer. Here are a few helpful hints for a perfect sauté:

1. Heat the pan and then add the fat. Your food will be less apt to stick.

2. Your food should be at room temperature and patted dry.

3. Parboil dense vegetables like carrots, potatoes, turnips and rutabagas if you're sautéing them with other quicker cooking vegetables like onions, celery, peppers or squash.

4. Salt slows the browning process. Season after sautéing if possible.

STEAMING

Steaming is one of the simplest and most nutritious ways to cook food. Unlike boiling, steaming will retain more of the food's vitamins and minerals. You can find a wide variety of steamers on the market but you may use a colander or sieve as well. To keep foods from becoming too wet, drape a towel over the basket before replacing the pot lid. This will keep the condensation that normally collects on the lid from falling back onto the food. This technique is particularly effective when you want light and puffy steamed rice.

STIR-FRYING

I use this term interchangeably with sautéing. It's simply the oriental method for cooking food quickly in a minimum amount of fat. Some cooks insist upon using a wok. If you already have one, by all means use it. But for the amount of food we will be cooking throughout this book, a good skillet or sauté pan will do just fine.

Ingredients

INGREDIENTS

BROTH/STOCK

Homemade broth is certainly hard to beat, but many of us don't have the time, inclination, or freezer space to create our own broth or stock from scratch. This is where a good soup base comes to the rescue. Available on-line and in many supermarkets, soup bases are seasoned, paste-style concentrates of freshly cooked meat, poultry, seafood and vegetables. There are several excellent soup bases and stocks on the market including, but not limited to, Tones, Minor's, Better than Bouillon, and Glory Foods. These are all superior to bouillon cubes, which you should avoid at all costs. Whatever brand you choose, be sure to examine the ingredients – the first item listed for beef base should be beef, chicken should be chicken, ham should be ham, and so on. You may be able to save additional money by purchasing larger containers of often-used base from one of the club stores, like Costco or Sam's. That's where I purchase my chicken and beef base.

BUTTER

Although this staple has gotten a bad rap for the last 30 or so years, I feel it is totally undeserved. When used in moderation and primarily as a flavoring, butter is a delicious addition to many dishes and will not be detrimental to your health. Those who still insist on margarine as a healthier alternative have not read the latest research. But remember, the key is to use it as a flavoring enhancer; for sautéing I recommend olive oil.

CAPERS

Sun-dried flower buds, which are usually pickled in brine and jarred, add a piquancy to any dish. Find them in the pickle section of your supermarket.

COCONUT MILK

Found canned or frozen in most supermarkets. Use unsweetened.

CREAM

I'm referring to half and half or regular whipping cream in the recipes that follow. Heavy whipping cream would be too thick.

HERBS & SPICES

Fresh or dried? It depends. I try to use fresh herbs when available but many times I have to rely on dried, when I use 1/3 the amount. Herbs with woody stems and strong aromatics, such as thyme and oregano, intensify in flavor once dried and may be used in many soups, stews, roasts and other cold-weather dishes. Summer herbs like parsley, cilantro, chives, and basil are best used fresh because they lose too much flavor when dried. Fresh herbs are best when added toward the end of a recipe while dried should be added toward the beginning. When using dried herbs, crumble them between your fingers to release their oils before you add them to your recipe. As far as spices go, most will be dried because fresh spices can be rare. Below are some recommendations:

Basil (best fresh)	Chives (best fresh)
Coriander Seeds (best dried)	Cumin (best dried)
Dill (best fresh)	Ginger (best fresh)
Oregano (best dried)	Parsley (best fresh)
Rosemary (fresh or dried)	Sage (fresh or dried)
Tarragon (best fresh)	Thyme (fresh or dried)
Turmeric (best dried)	

The recipes that follow use dried herbs, unless it is absolutely essential to use fresh, because this is what many of us have at our disposal. I do encourage you to use fresh whenever possible, just remember to triple the amount.

LEMON, LIME, AND ORANGE JUICE

You'll notice that I use quite a bit of citrus in my cooking. Living in Florida, who wouldn't? Hands down, fresh is optimal, but it is not always convenient. I keep some Minute Maid Frozen Lemon Juice® on hand when I'm in a pinch and avoid bottled lemon juice because the taste is substantially different from fresh. However, I do keep a bottle of Nellie and Joe's Key Lime Juice® in the fridge – it's a good substitute for fresh squeezed lime juice. When it comes to orange juice, I often opt for the not-from-concentrate bottled variety when I don't have any fresh oranges on hand. Ditto for grapefruit juice.

OILS

You'll find that I use olive oil in most of these recipes. It has a wonderful flavor and, because it is mono-unsaturated, it is easy on the heart. I use the less expensive 'pure' olive oil for basic sautéing and reserve extra virgin when I want the flavor of the oil to shine through. Of course, you may use canola oil in place of pure olive oil. I use other oils, like sesame and walnut, when I feel their distinctive flavor is necessary for the dish.

PINE NUTS

These expensive little nuggets actually come from a large species of pinecone in Italy. Like many nuts and seeds, their flavor improves with toasting.

PROSCIUTTO

This Italian ham has been seasoned and air-dried. Sliced razor thin, this richly delicious meat will go a long way. Buy in small batches from your butcher or in many supermarkets.

SHALLOTS

A cross between the garlic and the onion, these are sometimes unavailable. A simple mix of a little onion with garlic will yield a similar flavor.

VINEGARS

I try to keep a bottle of each of these in my cupboard:

Red Wine Vinegar	White Wine Vinegar
Cider Vinegar	Rice Wine Vinegar
Balsamic Vinegar	Malt Vinegar

These should do for most of the recipes you're likely to come across. As for the wide variety of flavored vinegars on the market, i.e. Tarragon Vinegar, I often make my own, which is cheaper, or I simply add that particular herb to the dish.

WINE

I have one simple rule when cooking with wine: If you can't drink it, don't cook with it. The cooking wines found next to the vinegar at the grocery store are loaded with salt. You're better off buying an inexpensive red or white wine from your wine merchant. This goes for Sherry, Madeira, and other fortified wines as well.

Soups

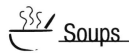 # Soups

Have you ever met anyone who didn't enjoy a bowl of homemade soup? Me neither. Nothing warms a body like a steaming bowl of soup or chowder on a chilly winter's night. Who could turn down a refreshing bowl of gazpacho when the midday summer sun forces us into the shade for lunch? In spring, summer, winter and fall, soup is the ultimate comfort food. It's healthy, economical, and downright convenient. I'm not talking about canned soup. Sure it's convenient and will do in a pinch, but it's not as economical as homemade and may not be as healthful as we would like. (Check the labels for salt, high fructose corn syrup, and additives). No, when I'm talking soup, I mean homemade. There was a time when making soup from scratch meant spending hours to make the broth - browning bones, then simmering the stock. But thanks to the many varieties of commercial soup bases available to the home cook (see the chapter on Ingredients) homemade soups are now possible for the table-for-two chef. Simply serve a few slices of fresh, crusty bread and a bowl of salad with your favorite soup to create a glorious and filling meal.

In the pages that follow, I've included recipes for time-honored traditional selections like chicken noodle soup and clam chowder, but I've also included some new favorites like bacon and tomato soup (for those who feel that a BLT sandwich is the ultimate in luncheon fare).

Oh, and by the way, I fudged a little on these recipes. They're for four. Why? Because as we all know, soup tastes better the next day.

• CHUNKY TOMATO POTATO SOUP •

I know you can buy tomato soup in a can, but once you try this hearty soup with cubes of tomatoes and potatoes swimming together in a rich stock with bits of carrot and celery, you may never go back. I've suggested using canned diced tomatoes, but if garden fresh ripe tomatoes are available, by all means use them. Serve this with a tossed salad and warm fresh bread for a quick late-October meal.

PREP: 20 minutes   COOK: 35 minutes

INGREDIENTS
  1 tablespoon unsalted butter
  1 medium onion, chopped
  2 cups peeled, cubed red potatoes
  3/4 cup chopped celery
  3/4 cup chopped carrots
  1 clove garlic, minced
  1-1/2 teaspoons Italian seasoning
  1 bay leaf
  1 cup milk
  1-1/2 teaspoons cornstarch
  1 (14.5-ounce) can diced tomatoes
  1/2 cup chicken or vegetable broth
  1 tablespoon tomato paste
  Salt and pepper to taste

DIRECTIONS
1.   Melt the butter in a medium saucepan over medium heat. Add the onions and sauté until soft and translucent, about 8 minutes. Add the garlic and sauté 1 additional minute. Mix in the potatoes, celery, and carrots. Season with Italian seasoning; add bay leaf and stir to blend.

2.   Pour in milk, gradually stir in cornstarch, and bring to a boil. Mix in tomatoes, broth, and tomato paste. Return to boil, reduce heat to low, and simmer 20 minutes. Season with salt and pepper.

• CHEDDAR CHEESE SOUP •

As a special treat, serve this in sourdough bread bowls.

PREP: 10 minutes   COOK: 35 minutes

INGREDIENTS:
    1 cup chicken or beef broth
    1 cup peeled and diced potatoes
    1/4 cup diced carrots
    1/4 cup chopped celery
    2 tablespoons chopped onions
    3/4 teaspoon kosher salt
    1/8 teaspoon ground black pepper
    1/2 cup cooked ham, cubed
    2 tablespoons unsalted butter
    2 tablespoons all-purpose flour
    1 cup milk
    1 cup shredded sharp Cheddar cheese
    Chopped fresh chives to garnish

DIRECTIONS:

1. Combine the broth, potatoes, carrots, celery, onions, salt, and pepper in a large saucepan. Bring to boil. Reduce heat and simmer 30 minutes, or until vegetables are tender.

2. Mix the ham into the vegetable mixture.

3. Melt the butter in a medium saucepan over medium heat. Stir in the flour until smooth and cooked. Slowly stir in the milk. Bring to a boil. Cook and stir for 2 minutes, or until thickened. Stir in the Cheddar cheese until melted.

4. Stir the melted cheese mixture in with the vegetable mixture, garnish with chopped chives, and serve.

• BAKED POTATO SOUP •

A steaming-hot baked potato topped with melted Cheddar cheese, crisp bacon bits, and freshly chopped chives is almost a meal in itself. When prepared as a soup, you have a meal indeed.

PREP: 10 minutes   COOK: 20 minutes

INGREDIENTS
  3 bacon strips, diced
  1 small onion, chopped
  1 clove garlic, minced
  3 tablespoons all-purpose flour
  1 teaspoon kosher salt
  1 teaspoon dried basil
  1/2 teaspoon freshly ground pepper
  3 cups chicken broth
  2 large baked potatoes, peeled and cubed
  1 cup half-and-half or light cream
  1/2 teaspoon hot pepper sauce
  Shredded Cheddar cheese
  Minced fresh parsley

DIRECTIONS
  1. Cook bacon in a large saucepan over medium-high heat until crisp. Drain, reserving 1 tablespoon drippings. Set bacon aside.

  2. Sauté onion until soft and translucent, about 8 minutes. Add garlic and sauté 1 additional minute. Stir in flour, salt, basil and pepper; mix well and cook about 5 minutes. Gradually stir in broth. Bring to boil. Stir for 2 or 3 minutes.

  3. Add the potatoes, cream and hot pepper sauce; heat through but do not boil. Garnish with bacon, cheese and parsley.

• BACON AND TOMATO SOUP •

I love BLT sandwiches. Who doesn't? This simple to prepare soup embodies the flavors that make the sandwich so outstanding. This recipe is inspired by one I saw many years ago in *The Complete Book of Soups and Stews* by Bernard Clayton. It's been a hit in my family ever since.

PREP: 5 minutes   COOK: 30 minutes

INGREDIENTS
   1 small onion, chopped
   2 strips bacon, diced
   1 tablespoon unsalted butter
   1 (14.5-ounce) can chopped tomatoes
   1/2 teaspoon thyme
   1 bay leaf
   2 cups vegetable or chicken stock
   Salt and pepper to taste
   1/4 cup heavy cream (or sour cream for a little bite)
   Chopped fresh parsley and ground nutmeg to garnish

DIRECTIONS
   1.   Melt the butter in a medium saucepan over medium heat. Sauté the onion and bacon until the onion is soft and the bacon is cooked. Add tomatoes, thyme, and bay leaf and cook for 5 - 6 minutes.

   2.   Add the stock and salt and pepper to taste. Bring to a boil, turn the heat to low and simmer for 20 minutes.

   3.   Remove the bay leaf and put the soup through a food mill, food processor or pulse in a blender.

   4.   Serve with a tablespoon of heavy cream and sprinkle with chopped parsley and ground nutmeg to garnish.

• IRISH CABBAGE SOUP •

People often ask why I have so many children. I tell them it's because I'm Irish. It's a requirement. They always respond, "You Irish must really love kids." Nonsense. We Irish really love sex. That, and cabbage soup.

PREP: 5 minutes   COOK: 1-1/2 hours

INGREDIENTS
1/2 cup chopped onions
1/2 cup diced celery
3 tablespoons unsalted butter, divided
1/2 pound cabbage
1-1/2 teaspoons minced fresh parsley
3 tablespoons all-purpose flour
4 cups chicken stock
4 red potatoes, cubed
6 thinly slice mushrooms
4 ounces frozen peas, defrosted
1/4 pound kielbasa, sliced 1/4 diagonal slice
Salt and pepper to taste

DIRECTIONS
1. Melt the 2 tablespoons butter in a large saucepan over medium heat. Sauté the onions and celery until tender and translucent, about 10 minutes.

2. Cut the cabbage lengthwise and remove the core. Slice into 3/8 inch shreds. Add the cabbage and parsley to the saucepan and cook for 10 minutes until the cabbage wilts.

3. Stir in the flour and cook for 3 minutes. Add the stock and potatoes and bring to a simmer. Stir well and cook for 30 minutes.

4. Meanwhile, melt remaining butter in a small skillet and sauté mushrooms until their moisture is released. Add the peas and heat through.

5. After the soup has cooked for 20 minutes, add the kielbasa, peas and mushrooms. Bring to a boil, reduce heat and simmer for 10 minutes. Add salt and pepper to taste.

• FRENCH ONION SOUP •

I know this looks like a lot of work for a bowl of soup – but once you savor it, you'll wonder why you ever enjoyed the onion soups found in most restaurants. Serve it as part of a larger meal, or simply enjoy it on a cold, winter's night with a loaf of French bread and a bottle of Cabernet.

PREP:10 minutes   COOK: 1 hour 45 minutes

INGREDIENTS
    2 tablespoons unsalted butter
    2 large onions, thinly sliced (about 2 cups)
    Salt to taste
    1/4 teaspoon sugar
    1 clove garlic, crushed
    1-1/2 teaspoons flour
    1/4 cup red wine
    2-1/2 cups beef broth
    Pinch of thyme
    1 teaspoon chopped fresh parsley
    1 small bay leaf
    2 tablespoons cognac or other good brandy
    1 loaf French bread
    4 slices Gruyere or Swiss cheese, 4 inches square and 1/8 inch thick

DIRECTIONS
1. Melt butter in a large saucepan over medium heat and add the onions, salt and sugar. Cover and sweat, stirring frequently, for 15 minutes, or until onions are tender and translucent.

2. Uncover and add garlic. Cook over medium heat until onions are a deep golden brown, about 20 to 30 minutes, stirring frequently. Stir in the flour and cook about 3 minutes.

3. Pour in the red wine and deglaze the pan, scraping up the brown bits from the bottom of the pan. Cook over medium-high heat until wine is nearly evaporated.

4. Add the stock, thyme, parsley and bay leaf. Partially cover and simmer for 45 minutes.

5. In the meantime, preheat oven to 325°. Cut two 1-inch thick slices of bread from the loaf. Butter and toast the bread slices just until browned, about 10 minutes. Reserve the remaining bread to serve with the soup.

6. Increase oven temperature to 375°. Place rack in center.

7. Fill two oven-proof 1-1/2 cup tureens with the soup. Add 1 tablespoon cognac to each bowl. Lay the toasted bread on top and seal each with 2 pieces of cheese. Bake for 10 to 15 minutes or until cheese has melted. Turn on broiler and broil until cheese is bubbly and golden-brown.

• HEARTY VEGETABLE BEEF SOUP •

I remember downing bowls of this hearty soup after skating on the thick ice of Mamaroneck harbor, just north of New York City, as a child. Now I live in Florida. I still make it often in the winter. We just watch the ice-skating on TV.

PREP: 10 minutes   COOK: 50 minutes

INGREDIENTS
   3/4 pound ground sirloin
   1/2 cup chopped onion
   1 clove garlic, minced
   1 (14.5-ounce) can stewed tomatoes
   2-1/2 cups beef broth
   1 teaspoon kosher salt
   1 carrot, chopped
   1 stalk celery, chopped
   1 russet potato, diced
   1/8 teaspoon dried thyme
   1 bay leaf
   1/2 teaspoon black pepper
   1/8 teaspoon dried basil

DIRECTIONS
   1. Brown sirloin, onion and garlic in a medium Dutch oven or large saucepan over medium heat. Drain grease and add tomatoes, broth, salt, carrots, celery, potatoes, thyme, bay leaf, pepper and basil. Cover and cook until vegetables are tender, about 30 minutes.

• MINESTRONE – MY WAY •

This famous Italian soup has as many variations as there are families who prepare it. Now I'd like to add my version to the mix. Try it this way, then experiment. Pretty soon you'll have your own version! And if you're able, make this a day ahead to truly enjoy the melding of the flavors.

PREP: 15 minutes   COOK: 1 hour

INGREDIENTS

3 tablespoons olive oil
1 leek, white part only, sliced
1 clove garlic, crushed
2 carrots, chopped
1 zucchini, diced
4 ounces green beans, cut into
   1-inch pieces
2 stalks celery, thinly sliced
1 red boiling potato, diced
1 quart beef stock
1 (15-ounce) can chopped tomatoes
1 tablespoon tomato paste
1 bay leaf

2 tablespoons chopped fresh
   parsley
1/2 teaspoon thyme
1/4 teaspoon oregano
1/4 teaspoon basil
1 (15-ounce) can cannellini
   beans, with liquid
1/4 cup elbow macaroni
Salt and ground black pepper
   to taste
Grated Parmesan cheese to
   garnish

DIRECTIONS

1. Heat olive oil in a medium Dutch oven or large saucepan over medium heat. Add leek, garlic, carrots, zucchini, green beans, celery and potato. Cover, and reduce heat to low. Cook for 15 minutes, shaking the pan occasionally.

2. Stir in the stock, tomatoes, tomato paste, bay leaf, parsley, thyme, oregano, and basil. Bring to a boil, cover and reduce heat to low; simmer gently for 30 minutes.

3. Stir in the cannellini beans with liquid and pasta. Simmer for an additional 10 minutes, or until pasta is al dente. Season with salt and pepper to taste.

4. Serve garnished with grated Parmesan cheese on top.

• MOM'S CHICKEN NOODLE SOUP •

Everyone's mom has a recipe for this soup. My mom often ladled out bowlfuls when we were stuck in bed with a cold. Bet your's did, too. Did it help? Many studies suggest that chicken soup does help break up congestion and eases the flow of nasal secretions. Many also say it inhibits white blood cells that trigger the inflammatory response, which causes sore throats and the production of phlegm. The chicken in the soup also contains an amino acid called cysteine. This thins mucus in the lungs, aiding in the healing process. So yeah, chicken soup alleviates cold symptoms. Besides, when did medicine taste so good?

PREP: 10 minutes   COOK: 25 minutes

INGREDIENTS
    2 teaspoons unsalted butter
    2 medium onions, diced
    2 ribs celery, chopped
    5 cups chicken broth
    5 ounces chopped cooked chicken breast
    1 cup egg noodles
    2 carrots, thinly sliced
    1/4 teaspoon dried basil
    1/4 teaspoon dried oregano
    Salt and pepper to taste

DIRECTIONS
1. Melt butter in a medium Dutch oven or a large saucepan over medium heat. Sauté onion and celery in butter until just tender, about 8 minutes.

2. Pour in chicken broth and stir in chicken, noodles, carrots, basil, oregano, salt and pepper. Bring to a boil. Reduce heat and simmer 20 minutes or until noodles are soft.

• CIOPPINO •

This wonderful Italian classic is more like a stew than a soup and this recipe will make plenty because you're sure to come back for seconds. Feel free to experiment with the amount and variety of seafood depending on what is available. No scallops? Double the amount of shrimp. Calamari on hand? Add it! The key is to use as much fresh seafood as possible. I use shelled steamed snow crab legs in place of canned – a little more work but worth the effort if you have the time.

PREP: 10 minutes   COOK: 45 minutes

INGREDIENTS

4 tablespoons unsalted butter
1 onion, chopped
1 clove garlic, minced
1/4 cup chopped fresh parsley
(14.5-ounce) can stewed tomatoes
1-1/2 cups chicken broth
1 bay leaf
1 teaspoon dried basil
1/2 teaspoon dried oregano
1/2 teaspoon dried thyme
1/4 cup clam juice or water
1/2 cup dry white wine

1/2 pound large shrimp –
    peeled and deveined
6 ounces lump crabmeat –
    fresh if possible, but
    canned will do
1/2 pound bay scallops
8 small clams (or one 10-oz.
    can chopped clams)
8 mussels, cleaned and
    de-bearded
8-ounces cod fillets, cubed
    (optional)

DIRECTIONS

1. Melt butter in a medium Dutch oven or large saucepan over medium heat. Add onions and sauté until they are soft and translucent, about 10 minutes. Add garlic and parsley and sauté an additional minute.

2. Add tomatoes to the pot (break them into chunks as you add them). Add chicken broth, bay leaf, basil, oregano, thyme, clam juice and wine. Mix well. Cover and simmer 30 minutes.

3. Stir in the shrimp, scallops, clams, mussels and crabmeat. Stir in fish, if desired. Bring to boil. Lower heat, cover and simmer 5 to 7 minutes until clams and mussels open. Ladle soup into warm bowls.

Serve with lots of warm, crusty bread and a bottle of Sauvignon Blanc or Pinot Grigio.

• CLASSIC NEW ENGLAND CLAM CHOWDER •

I grew up on Long Island Sound and every weekend our home overflowed with aunts, uncles, cousins, and friends. In the morning my Uncle Charlie would take all the kids out to the flats to dig for clams. We'd return with pails filled to the brim. Then we'd run off to play while the adults attended to the shucking. By mid-afternoon we'd find ourselves scattered across the patio and lawn with steaming bowls of chowder balanced on our laps. Here's Uncle Charlie's recipe using canned clams and pared down for the Table for Two kitchen.

PREP: 15 minutes   COOK: 30 minutes

INGREDIENTS
2/3 cup chopped onion
2 cloves garlic
Water (or bottled clam juice)
3 cups peeled and diced boiling potatoes
2/3 cup diced celery
3/4 teaspoon kosher salt
1/4 teaspoon ground black pepper
2 (10-ounce) cans minced clams, drained with juice reserved
2-2/3 cups half-and-half cream
1/4 teaspoon white sugar
1/2 cup unsalted butter, melted
1/2 cup all-purpose flour

DIRECTIONS

1. Combine onion, garlic and enough water/clam juice to make a smooth paste. Set aside.

2. Combine potatoes, celery, salt, pepper, onion mixture, and juice from clams in a medium Dutch oven or large saucepan. Augment with enough water/clam juice to cover. Bring to a boil, then reduce heat and simmer until potatoes are soft, about 15 minutes.

3. Meanwhile, melt butter in a small saucepan over medium-high heat. Stir in the flour and whisk for 5 minutes to make a roux.

4. Stir half-and-half and sugar into the soup. Then slowly whisk the roux into soup. Cook and stir until thickened. Stir in clams and adjust seasonings.

• CREAMY SCALLOP CHOWDER •

For a seafood chowder, you won't go wrong with this sumptuous soup featuring white wine, onions, and tender scallops. You may use either ocean or bay scallops, but if you use ocean, be sure to cut them in quarters.

PREP: 10 minutes   COOK: 20 minutes

INGREDIENTS
    1 pound scallops, rinsed and drained
    2 tablespoons unsalted butter
    1 bunch green onion, minced
    4 ounces fresh mushrooms, sliced
    2 tablespoons all-purpose flour
    1 cup milk
    1/2 cup dry white wine
    1 teaspoon kosher salt
    1 pinch ground white pepper
    1/2 cup shredded Swiss cheese
    2 tablespoons chopped fresh parsley

DIRECTIONS
    1.   Wash and drain scallops.

    2.   Melt butter in a large saucepan, over medium-low heat. Sauté onions and mushrooms until tender, about 10 to 15 minutes.

    3.   Stir in flour and cook for 3 to 5 minutes. Pour in milk and stir over medium heat until thickened and bubbly. Add wine, scallops, salt and pepper. Cook over medium heat until thickened. Serve topped with Swiss cheese and parsley.

• SALMON CHOWDER •

While clam chowder always receives top billing, this variation is a nice twist. This savory chowder can be made with 1 pound of any firm-fleshed fish.

PREP: 15 minutes   COOK: 30 minutes

INGREDIENTS
2 tablespoons unsalted butter
1/2 cup chopped onion
1/4 cup chopped celery
1 clove garlic, minced
1 cup diced red potatoes
1 carrot, diced
1 cup chicken broth
1/2 teaspoon kosher salt
1/2 teaspoon ground black pepper
1/2 teaspoon dried dill weed
1 (16-ounce) can salmon or 1 pound salmon fillet
1 (12-ounce) can evaporated milk
1 (15-ounce) can creamed corn
1 cup Cheddar cheese, shredded

DIRECTIONS
1. Melt butter in a large saucepan over medium heat. Sauté onions and celery until soft, about 10 minutes. Add garlic and sauté 1 additional minute. Stir in potatoes, carrots, broth, salt, pepper, and dill. Bring to a boil, and reduce heat. Cover, and simmer 20 minutes.

2. Stir in salmon, evaporated milk, corn, and cheese. Cook until heated through.

Serve with toasted sourdough bread.

• PENNSYLVANIA DUTCH CORN CHOWDER •

My wife is of German extract and hails from Pennsylvania Dutch country. This is her contribution to our Scots-Irish household. I'll take it over haggis soup any day.

PREP: 5 minutes   COOK: 30 minutes

INGREDIENTS
  4 slices bacon, diced
  2 medium potatoes, peeled and chopped
  1 medium onion, chopped
  1 cup chicken stock
  1-1/2 cups cream-style corn
  1 teaspoon kosher salt
  Salt and pepper to taste
  1 cup half-and-half

DIRECTIONS
1. Place the bacon in a medium Dutch oven or large saucepan over medium-high heat, and cook until crisp. Drain and crumble, reserving about 1 tablespoon drippings in the pot.

2. Mix potatoes and onion into the pot with the crumbled bacon and reserved drippings. Cook and stir 5 minutes. Add the stock and stir in corn. Season with salt and pepper. Bring to a boil, reduce heat to low, cover pot and simmer 15 minutes, stirring frequently, until potatoes are tender.

3. Meanwhile, warm the half-and-half in a small saucepan until it bubbles. Remove from heat before it boils, and mix into the chowder just before serving.

• HEARTY VEGETABLE CHOWDER •

There are many variations to this traditional recipe. I've included one that uses fresh cauliflower, carrots, and broccoli. In a pinch you may use a frozen California Blend medley. For that matter, feel free to use any variety of vegetables that you have on hand or in the freezer.

PREP: 15 minutes   COOK: 35 minutes

INGREDIENTS
- 1/4 cup chopped red bell pepper
- 1/4 cup chopped onion
- 2 tablespoons unsalted butter
- 1/2 cup chopped celery
- 1/2 cup cauliflower, chopped
- 1/2 cup diced carrots
- 1/2 cup fresh chopped broccoli (or 1-1/2 cups frozen cauliflower/carrot/ broccoli medley)
- 1-2/3 cups chicken broth or vegetable broth
- 1/4 cup all-purpose flour
- 3/4 cup milk
- 2 teaspoons chopped fresh parsley
- 1-2/3 cups shredded Cheddar cheese
- Salt and pepper to taste

DIRECTIONS

1. Heat the butter in a medium Dutch oven or large saucepan over medium-high heat. Sauté the pepper and onions until tender, about 8 minutes.

2. Add remaining vegetables, broth, salt, and pepper and bring to a boil. Reduce heat; cover and simmer and for 20 minutes, or until the vegetables are tender.

3. In a small bowl, whisk the flour and milk until smooth. Stir into pot and bring soup to a boil; cook and stir for 2 minutes. Mix in the parsley. Just before serving, stir in the cheese until melted.

• OYSTER STEW •

If you're a true oyster lover, then this soup is for you. If you're up to it, buy your own oysters and shuck them. Of course, if you're like me, you'll eat them as they're shucked and there won't be any left for the stew. So feel free to use the pints of oysters from your fish market or the refrigerated seafood section of your grocery store. But by no means should you use canned oysters. They simply will not do.

PREP: 5 minutes   COOK: 15 minutes

INGREDIENTS
    1 pint oysters with their liquor (about 2 cups)
    3 cups light cream
    1 cup milk
    Pinch cayenne pepper
    1/2 teaspoon kosher salt, or to taste
    4 tablespoons unsalted butter, divided
    Sweet paprika
    Chopped fresh parsley to garnish

DIRECTIONS
1. Pour liquor from oysters and reserve.

2. Scald the milk in small saucepan over medium-high heat.

3. Combine the milk with the cream, cayenne pepper, and salt in a small bowl.

4. Melt 2 tablespoons butter in a medium saucepan over medium heat and add the oysters. Cook, stirring occasionally, until the oysters are plump, about 5 minutes.

5. Pour the reserved oyster liquor and the cream mixture into the pan. Simmer, stirring gently, until the oysters begin to curl, about 5 minutes.

6. Ladle the stew into heated bowls, dot with remaining butter, sprinkle with paprika and garnish with parsley.

• BLACK BEAN AND SHRIMP BISQUE •

I've always loved black bean soup. It's such a simple and hearty dish. Here we take it up a notch with the addition of shrimp. This is good enough for company.

PREP: 10 minutes   COOK: 1 hour

INGREDIENTS
   1 can black beans, drained
   2 tablespoons olive oil
   1/2 cup chopped onion
   1 large carrot, coarsely grated
   1 stalk celery, diced
   1 clove garlic, crushed
   1/4 teaspoon basil
   1/4 teaspoon oregano
   1/4 teaspoon thyme
   1 medium tomato, peeled, cored and diced
   2 cups shrimp or chicken broth
   1/2 teaspoon kosher salt
   1/4 teaspoon freshly ground pepper
   1/4 pound cooked shrimp
   2 tablespoons sherry
   1 tablespoon chopped fresh parsley

DIRECTIONS
1. Heat oil in a medium Dutch oven or large saucepan over medium heat and sauté the onions, carrots and celery until very tender, about 15 minutes. Add the garlic, basil, oregano and thyme and sauté an additional 3 – 5 minutes.

2. Add the tomatoes, broth, salt and pepper, cover and simmer for 15 minutes.

3. Stir in beans and simmer an additional 15 minutes. Stir in shrimp and sherry and reheat to steaming (do not boil) about 3 more minutes.

Salads

 **Salads**

A recent UCLA/Louisiana State University study published in the Journal of the American Dietetic Association shows that a consumption of salad and raw vegetables correlates with higher concentrations of folic acid, vitamins C and E, lycopene and alpha and beta carotene in the bloodstream.

Mom was right. Eat your salad and your vegetables.

It's a good thing that salads are so easy to prepare. In your average supermarket you will find a dozen leafy greens available year round - everything from the old standbys like iceberg and Boston lettuce to more gourmet varieties like radicchio and arugula. Add to that the variety of highly nutritious greens like spinach, mustard greens, and collards and you will have enough choices to create a variety of salads for months. Many supermarkets offer pre-bagged selections; that can be a real boon for the Table for Two cook.

The key to a good green salad, apart from fresh greens, is the quality of the dressing. There are many excellent salad dressings available in today's market. Here is a basic recipe for a vinaigrette that's sure to please anyone's palate:

1 clove garlic, crushed
1/2 teaspoon kosher salt
1/4-cup quality balsamic vinegar (or quality red or white wine vinegar)
1/2 teaspoon Dijon-style mustard
3/4-cup quality extra-virgin olive oil
2 teaspoons minced shallot (optional)
Freshly ground black pepper to taste

Mix the garlic and salt in a small bowl to create a paste. Stir in the vinegar and mustard then drizzle the olive oil, whisking as you go. Stir in the shallots and black pepper.

Since creating a tossed green salad with a flavorful dressing is easier than ever, I've focused on salads that move beyond simple greens and dressings for a delightfully different change of pace. Experiment and enjoy!

• BROCCOLI BACON SALAD •

PREP: 10 minutes   COOK: 15 minutes
CHILL: 2 + hours

INGREDIENTS
3 slices bacon   1 cup broccoli florets
1 tablespoon chopped red onion   1/3 cup mayonnaise
1 tablespoon white wine vinegar   2 teaspoons sugar
1/3 cup sunflower seeds
2 tablespoons halved red seedless grapes

DIRECTIONS

Place bacon in a skillet. Cook over medium high heat until crisp and brown. Drain, crumble and set aside. Combine the broccoli, onion, and grapes in a medium bowl. In a small bowl, whisk together the vinegar, sugar and mayonnaise. Pour over broccoli mixture, and toss. Cover and refrigerate for at least two hours. Toss salad with crumbled bacon and sunflower seeds and serve.

• GRAPEFRUIT WITH SHRIMP •

PREP: 10 minutes   CHILL: 30 minutes

INGREDIENTS
1 grapefruit, halved
12 cooked tiny shrimp or 6 medium shrimp, halved
1/4 avocado, sliced thin crosswise
Balsamic Vinaigrette (see page 30)
Arugula or watercress springs, for garnish

DIRECTIONS

Remove seeds from the grapefruit and cut around the sections with a knife. While holding the fruit over a bowl to catch the juice, remove alternate sections of grapefruit fruit and save for another use. Toss the avocado with the juice. Insert a shrimp and avocado slice in each space. Drizzle with the vinaigrette and place a sprig of greenery in the center of each grapefruit half. Serve chilled.

• SLICED TOMATOES WITH BASIL •

PREP: 10 minutes   SET: 1 hour

INGREDIENTS
    2 ripe tomatoes sliced 1/4 inch thick
    1 teaspoon sugar
    1/4 teaspoon kosher salt
    Pinch of black pepper
    1 tablespoon balsamic vinegar
    2 tablespoons extra virgin olive oil
    2 tablespoons chopped fresh basil

DIRECTIONS

Arrange tomato slices in an overlapping circle on a plate. Sprinkle with the sugar, salt, pepper and vinegar. Cover loosely with waxed paper and let sit at room temp for 1 to 1-1/2 hours. Drizzle with olive oil and sprinkle with basil and serve.

• SPRING SPINACH AND STRAWBERRY SALAD •

PREP: 10 minutes

INGREDIENTS
    1 bunch spinach, rinsed and torn into bite-size pieces
    1 cup sliced strawberries
    2 tablespoons olive oil
    1 tablespoon white wine vinegar
    2 tablespoons white sugar
    1/8 teaspoon sweet paprika
    1-1/2 teaspoons sesame seeds
    3/4 teaspoon poppy seeds

DIRECTIONS

Toss together the spinach and strawberries in a bowl. Whisk together the oil, vinegar, sugar, paprika, sesame seeds, and poppy seeds in a small bowl. Pour over the spinach and strawberries, and toss to coat.

• CRAB AND SHRIMP SALAD •

PREP: 10 minutes   CHILL: 1 hour

INGREDIENTS

1/4 pound fresh crabmeat, drained and flaked
1/4 pound small cooked shrimp, chopped
1/2 stalk celery, diced
1/2 green bell pepper, seeded and chopped
1/2 onion, diced
1/4 cup and 2 tablespoons mayonnaise
1 teaspoon fresh dill, finely chopped
1/2 teaspoon Worcestershire sauce
Salt and ground black pepper to taste
Fresh green lettuce

DIRECTIONS

Toss the crabmeat, shrimp, celery, bell pepper, and onion together in a bowl. Stir in the mayonnaise, dill, and Worcestershire sauce until evenly blended. Season to taste with salt and pepper. Refrigerate 1 hour before serving over lettuce.

• SEAFOOD PASTA SALAD •

PREP: 20 minutes   CHILL: 2 hours

INGREDIENTS

1 teaspoon unsalted butter
1/4 pound fresh shrimp,
   peeled and deveined
1/4 pound lump crabmeat
1/4 cup mayonnaise
2-1/4 teaspoons fresh lemon juice
1-1/2 teaspoons chopped fresh parsley
1/4 green onion, thinly sliced

1/4 cup shredded
   mozzarella cheese
1 tablespoon slivered,
   toasted almonds
2 ounces seashell pasta
1/2 strip celery, sliced
1/4 red bell pepper, chopped
1/4 teaspoon Old Bay® Seasoning

DIRECTIONS

1. Melt the butter in a small skillet over medium heat and sauté shrimp until pink. Add crabmeat and cook one more minute or until heated through. Set aside in a serving bowl.

2. Bring a pot of lightly salted water to a boil. Add pasta and cook for 8 to 10 minutes or until al dente; drain.

3. Add pasta, celery, bell pepper and green onion to the crab and shrimp Add mozzarella cheese, slivered toasted almonds, mayonnaise, and lemon juice. Season with parsley and Old Bay® Seasoning. Toss to mix thoroughly.

4. Refrigerate for 2 hours before serving. Serve on a small bed of greens.

• PEAR AND ROQUEFORT SALAD •

PREP: 20 minutes   COOK: 10 minutes

INGREDIENTS

2 teaspoons water
1 tablespoon plus 1/2 teaspoon
    white sugar, divided
2-1/2 tablespoons pecans
2 tablespoons olive oil
1 tablespoon red wine vinegar
1/2 teaspoon Dijon mustard
1 clove garlic, minced
1/8 teaspoon kosher salt
Fresh ground black pepper to taste

2 cups torn leaf lettuce
1 ripe pear, peeled, cored and
    chopped
1-1/2 ounces Roquefort or other
    blue cheese, crumbled
1 ripe avocado - peeled, pitted,
    and diced
2-1/2 tablespoons thinly sliced
    green onions

DIRECTIONS

1. Heat the water in a small skillet over medium heat and stir in 1 tablespoon of sugar together with the pecans. Continue stirring gently until sugar has melted and caramelized the pecans. Transfer nuts onto waxed paper. Allow to cool, then break into pieces.

2. Combine olive oil, vinegar, 1/2 teaspoon sugar, mustard, minced garlic, salt, and pepper in a small bowl.

3. Layer the lettuce, pears, blue cheese, avocado, and green onions on a serving plate. Pour dressing over salad, sprinkle with pecans, and serve.

Seafood

Seafood

We all know that seafood is integral to a healthy and balanced diet. Many recent studies show that increasing our seafood consumption and variety will have a positive effect on our health. According to *The Journal of the American Medical Association*, eating fish reduces the risk of coronary death by 36 percent. This is why the American Heart Association recommends two servings of fish each week.

In the pages that follow, I offer a varied and delicious collection of seafood recipes using readily available fish and shellfish. I think one of the reasons we shy away from preparing seafood more often is the sheer variety that is cited in cookbooks and available at the fish market. After all, there are over 25,000 different types of fish in the world – that's more than mammals, reptiles, amphibians and birds – combined! How many of us know the difference between snow crab and king crab? Chilean sea bass and rockfish? Sculp or amberjack? And what the heck is crappie anyway?

I hope this chapter will help you navigate through the range of choices available at your market. I've tried to include fish that are fairly common in all parts of the country. If you find a recipe that sounds intriguing, but the particular fish is unavailable, feel free to substitute using the chart below:

Grouper: striped bass, black sea bass (flakier texture), mahi-mahi, pompano, lemonfish, catfish, red snapper (flakier texture).

Mahi-mahi: orange roughy, red snapper, swordfish, tuna, catfish (fattier), tilefish (flakier texture, not as sweet), monkfish (not as sweet),

Tuna: swordfish, sturgeon, marlin, halibut, salmon, kingfish, mackerel.

Cod: Pollock, halibut, sole, flounder, orange roughy, haddock, whiting, ocean perch, tilapia.

Flounder: sole, orange roughy, cod, haddock, tilapia.

Orange roughy: flounder, sole, red snapper, ocean perch, grouper.

Salmon: swordfish, mahi-mahi, albacore tuna, marlin, striped bass, trout.

Swordfish: tuna, halibut, marlin, mahi-mahi.

Snapper: sea bass, striped bass, grouper, rockfish.

A Special Note about Shrimp: In the shrimp recipes that follow, I suggest using 1 pound shell-on shrimp because you'll lose a bit of weight with shelling. If you purchase the shrimp already shelled, figure on 12 ounces. But then again, we're big shrimp-eaters in our house so 1 pound of shell-on shrimp is always the minimum. Should you desire less shrimp, the marinade and sauce amounts will remain the same.

• BAKED COD WITH SALSA •

Serve this with rice, black beans, warm tortillas and Margaritas, for a flavorful and festive south-of-the-border meal.

PREP: 5 minutes   COOK: 30 minutes

INGREDIENTS
  2 (4 to 6 ounce) cod fillets
  1 cup salsa – mild or spicy depending on taste
  1/3 cup shredded cheddar cheese
  1 tablespoon chopped fresh cilantro
  1/4 cup crushed tortilla chips
  1 avocado - peeled, pitted and sliced
  2 tablespoons sour cream
  Salt and pepper to taste

DIRECTIONS
  1. Preheat oven to 400 °.

  2. Rinse and dry cod fillets. Place fillets in a lightly greased casserole dish and sprinkle with salt and pepper to taste. Pour salsa over fish. Sprinkle with cheese and cilantro then tortilla chips.

  3. Bake for 12 -15 minutes until fish flakes easily with a fork. Serve topped with sliced avocado and sour cream.

Serve with Steamed White Rice and Cuban Black Beans

• BAKED COD WITH CILANTRO AND LIME •

Wrapping a fillet in foil or parchment paper prior to baking, referred to as *en papillote*, steams the fish and renders a tender and succulent entrée. The marriage of cilantro and lime adds a light and cleansing taste to this mildly flavored fish. Try this with the stronger tasting salmon for a nice change.

PREP: 5 minutes   COOK: 40 minutes

INGREDIENTS
   2 (4 to 6 oz) cod fillets
   1/8 teaspoon freshly ground pepper
   2 teaspoons olive oil
   1 tablespoon minced onion
   1 garlic clove, minced
   1/2 teaspoon ground cumin
   1 tablespoon minced fresh cilantro
   1/2 of a lime, thinly sliced
   2 teaspoons unsalted butter, melted

DIRECTIONS
   1.   Preheat oven to 375 °.

   2.   Place each fillet on a 12-in. x 12-in. piece of heavy-duty foil. Sprinkle with pepper.

   3.   Heat oil in a small skillet over medium-high heat. Add onion and sauté for 5 minutes. Add garlic and sauté 1 additional minute. Stir in cumin then spoon over fillets and sprinkle with cilantro. Place lime slices over each fillet and drizzle with melted butter.

   4.   Fold foil around fish and seal tightly. Place on a baking sheet and bake at 375° for 35-40 minutes or until fish flakes easily with a fork.

Serve with Buttered Noodles and Corn.

• BAKED COD WITH PARMESAN CHEESE •

This is certainly one recipe that requires the richness of extra virgin olive oil.

PREP: 5 minutes   COOK: 15 minutes

INGREDIENTS
    2 tablespoons dry white wine or chicken broth
    2 (4 - 6 ounce) cod fillets, cut into 1-inch pieces
    1/4 cup crushed saltine crackers
    1 teaspoon Italian herbs
    1 clove garlic, minced
    1/4 teaspoon sweet paprika
    2 teaspoons extra virgin olive oil
    2 teaspoons grated Parmesan cheese

DIRECTIONS

1.   Preheat oven to 400 °.

2.   Lightly butter a small baking dish. Pour in wine and add fish.

3.   Combine cracker crumbs, Italian herbs, garlic, and paprika in a small
      bowl then sprinkle over fish. Drizzle with oil and sprinkle with cheese.
      Bake, uncovered, at 400° for 12-15 minutes or until lightly browned
      and fish flakes easily with a fork.

Serve with Sautéed New Potatoes and Sautéed Glazed Tomatoes.

• SAUTÉED SPANISH COD •

Some people will refer to this as fried fish. Not me. Frying denotes cooking with fat that covers, or nearly covers, the item being cooked. Here we have a mere 2 teaspoons of fat, just enough to soften the onions while adding flavor. I've used whole fillets in this recipe and paired it with roasted red potatoes but you may also cut the fillets into 1½-inch chunks and serve this dish over steamed white rice.

PREP: 20 minutes   COOK: 15 minutes

INGREDIENTS
   1 teaspoon unsalted butter
   1 teaspoon olive oil
   2 tablespoons finely chopped onion
   2 teaspoons chopped fresh garlic
   1/3 cup tomato sauce
   2 plum tomatoes, peeled and diced
   3 tablespoons chopped green olives
   2 tablespoon coarsely chopped roasted red peppers (or pimentos)
   1/8 teaspoon black pepper
   1/8 teaspoon cayenne pepper
   1/8 teaspoon sweet paprika
   2 (4 - 6 ounce) cod fillets

DIRECTIONS
   1.   Heat butter and olive oil in a 10-inch skillet over medium heat. Add onions and sauté until soft and translucent, about 8 minutes. Add the garlic and sauté 1 additional minute.

   2.   Add tomato sauce and tomatoes and bring to a simmer. Stir in green olives and roasted peppers. Season with black pepper, cayenne pepper, and paprika. Reduce heat to medium.

   3.   Add fillets to sauce and cook for 5 - 8 minutes, or until easily flaked with a fork.

Serve with Roasted Red Potatoes and Garlic and Steamed Asparagus.

• SUCCULENT SEAFOOD MEDLEY •

This is one dish that is bursting with the flavors of the sea. Yes, it is rich and you shouldn't eat it every night, but for that rare special occasion it is hard to beat. Feel free to experiment with a mix of seafood. I've made this with a number of combinations: lobster meat, fresh-shucked oysters, clams, and mussels. Another addition? Shredded smoked provolone – nice!

PREP: 10 minutes   COOK: 20 minutes

INGREDIENTS
    2 (4 – 6 ounce) cod fillets, cut in half
    10 bay scallops
    3/4 cup lump crabmeat (2 6- ounce cans)
    10 medium shrimp, cooked
    1/2 cup shredded Monterey Jack cheese
    1/2 cup unsalted butter
    2 egg yolks
    1 tablespoon lemon juice
    1 tablespoon white wine
    1/2 teaspoon mustard powder
    1/8 teaspoon kosher salt
    2 tablespoons chopped fresh parsley
    1/4 teaspoon sweet paprika

DIRECTIONS
1.   Preheat oven to 450 °.

2.   Butter two 2-cup au gratin dishes. Place 1/2 fillet on bottom of each, then layer with scallops, crabmeat, shrimp, cheese and second 1/2 fillet; set aside.

3.   Melt butter. In a small bowl, combine yolks, lemon juice, white wine, mustard and salt. Whisk in melted butter and stir until sauce is thick and creamy. Pour sauce over fillets.

4.   Bake for 15 - 20 minutes. Sprinkle with parsley and paprika.

Serve with Rice Pilaf and Broccoli with Garlic Butter.

• SOLE IN LEMON-BUTTER SAUCE •

This and several subsequent recipes call for sole fillets. Truth be told, there is no sole in American waters. The sole we find in our local markets and restaurants are most likely members of the flounder family. Some fish mongers may import true sole from England, Belgium or the Netherlands but they will charge you a significant amount for their efforts. Not to worry. The following recipes will work just as well for flounder as they will sole.

PREP: 10 minutes   COOK: 20 minutes

INGREDIENTS
   2 (4 - 6 ounce) sole fillets
   1 egg, beaten
   1/2 cup dry bread crumbs
   1 tablespoon shredded Parmesan cheese
   2 cups olive oil for frying
   1/2 cup unsalted butter
   1 clove garlic, crushed
   1/2 cup chicken broth
   2 tablespoons white wine
   1/2 lemon, juiced
   Salt and pepper to taste
   1-1/2 teaspoons chopped fresh parsley

DIRECTIONS

1. Dip fillets in beaten egg, then in breadcrumbs, then in Parmesan.

2. Heat oil in a 10-inch skillet over medium-high heat to 375 °. Fry fish until golden brown. Transfer to a dish, and keep warm.

3. Melt butter in a small saucepan over medium heat. Add garlic and sauté 1 - 2 minutes. Stir in chicken broth, wine, and lemon juice; bring to a boil. Season with salt and pepper. Remove from heat, and stir in chopped parsley. Serve butter sauce over fish fillets.

Serve with Buttered Noodles with Carrots and Poppy Seeds.

• SAUTÉED SOLE WITH TOMATOES AND GREEN PEPPERS •

Fresh, ripe tomatoes are ideal for this recipe, but canned may be substituted if the tomatoes at the market are not fully ripe.

PREP: 5 minutes   COOK: 25 minutes

INGREDIENTS
   1 tablespoon olive oil
   1/2 cup chopped onion
   1/4 cup chopped green pepper
   1/2 cup diced tomatoes with juice
   3 teaspoons chopped parsley or 1-1/2 teaspoons dried
   1/2 teaspoon kosher salt
   1/2 teaspoon dried oregano
   2 (4 - 6 ounce) sole or flounder fillets

DIRECTIONS

1.   Heat olive oil in a 10-inch skillet over medium heat. Sauté onion and green pepper until onion is soft and translucent and the peppers are tender, about 8 minutes.

2.   Stir in the tomato juice, parsley, salt, and oregano and sauté for 5 minutes or until heated through.

3.   Add fillets. Cover and cook over medium heat for 12-15 minutes or until fish flakes easily with a fork.

Serve with Oven Fries and Roasted Garlic Cauliflower.

• FILLET OF SOLE WITH SHRIMP SAUCE •

The depth and richness of this dish belies its simplicity. Feel free to use 6 ounces of lump crab meat (canned is fine) instead of the shrimp. Simply place two teaspoons on each fillet and add the remainder to the sauce.

PREP: 10 minutes   COOK: 20 minutes

INGREDIENTS
   2 (4 - 6 ounce) sole or flounder fillets
   1 teaspoon lemon juice
   1/2 teaspoon kosher salt, divided
   1/8 teaspoon freshly ground pepper
   1/4 pound medium shrimp, peeled and de-veined
   1 tablespoon unsalted butter
   1 tablespoon all-purpose flour
   1/2 cup milk
   2 teaspoons Dijon mustard
   1/8 teaspoon white pepper

DIRECTIONS
   1.   Preheat oven to 425°.

   2.   Sprinkle each flounder fillet with lemon juice, 1/4 teaspoon salt, and pepper. Roll each fillet around a shrimp and secure with a toothpick. Chop remaining shrimp; set aside.

   3.   Rub 1 teaspoon butter in a small baking dish (or use a non-stick spray). Arrange rolled fillets seam side down in the dish. Cover and bake at 425 ° for 20-25 minutes or until fish flakes easily with a fork and shrimp turn pink.

   4.   Meanwhile, melt butter in a small saucepan over medium heat. Add flour and stir for a few minutes until well mixed. Gradually stir in the milk. Whisk in mustard, white pepper, and remaining salt until blended. Add remaining shrimp and bring to a boil; cook and stir for 1-2 minutes or until thickened and shrimp turn pink. Serve sauce over fish.

Serve with Rice and Peas.

• BAKED SOLE WITH FRESH TOMATO •

Try this when the tomatoes are bursting with flavor at the farmer's market. This is perfect for a late-spring or mid-summer meal.

PREP: 10 minutes   COOK: 15 minutes

INGREDIENTS
    2 small onions, thinly sliced
    2 tablespoons olive oil
    2 (4 - 6 ounce) sole or flounder fillets
    1/4 teaspoon kosher salt
    1/8 teaspoon freshly ground pepper
    2 plum tomatoes, sliced
    1/4 cup melted unsalted butter
    1/4 teaspoon garlic salt
    1/4 cup minced fresh parsley

DIRECTIONS
1.   Preheat oven to 350°.

2.   Heat olive oil in a 10-inch skillet over medium heat. Sauté onion until soft and translucent, about 8 minutes. Transfer to a buttered baking dish. Place fillets on top of onions. Sprinkle with salt and pepper. Top with tomato slices. Combine butter and garlic salt; pour over tomato. Sprinkle with parsley.

3.   Bake, uncovered for 14-18 minutes or until fish flakes easily with a fork.

Serve with a Tossed Green Salad and Buttered Noodles with Nutmeg.

• GRILLED SALMON STEAKS •

When my doctor advised me to cut back on red meat a number of years ago, I thought I was doomed. After all, I was a tried and true steak and baked potato lover. I began to prepare myself for what I assumed would be years of dining on tofu steaks, not that there is anything wrong with tofu, as long as it's prepared as tofu and not as a substitute for something that it plainly isn't. Then I discovered grilled salmon steak. I still enjoy a good beef steak on occasion, but this healthy alternative has moved to the top tier of my grilled favorites. It's hard to believe that something that tastes this good can be so good for you.

PREP: 5 minutes   COOK: 8 minutes

INGREDIENTS
   2 (4 - 6 ounce) salmon steaks
   1 tablespoon melted unsalted butter or olive oil
   1 tablespoon soy sauce
   1/8 teaspoon dried dill weed
   Lemon pepper to taste

DIRECTIONS
1. Preheat grill or oven broiler. Lightly grease a grill or baking sheet.

2. Place salmon on the baking sheet. Mix the melted butter, soy sauce, and dill weed in a small bowl. Brush mixture over salmon then sprinkle with lemon pepper.

3. Broil salmon 3 to 5 minutes per side, depending on thickness, or until easily flaked with a fork (do not over-cook).

Serve with Garlic Smashed Potatoes and Carrots in Dill

• MAPLE GLAZED SALMON FILLETS •

This is one time when buying real Vermont maple syrup makes all the difference in the world. It's expensive, I know, when compared to maple-flavored syrup, but you can use the imitation maple varieties on your pancakes and save the real thing for dishes like this.

PREP: 10 minutes   MARINATE: 30 minutes
COOK: 20 minutes

INGREDIENTS
    2 tablespoons maple syrup
    1 tablespoon soy sauce
    1 clove garlic, minced
    1/8 teaspoon kosher salt
    1/8 teaspoon ground black pepper
    2 (4 - 6 ounce) salmon fillets

DIRECTIONS

1. Preheat oven to 400°.

2. Combine the maple syrup, soy sauce, garlic, salt, and pepper in a small bowl.

3. Place salmon in a small shallow glass baking dish and coat with the maple syrup mixture. Cover and marinate salmon in the refrigerator for 30 minutes, turning once.

4. Place the baking dish in the preheated oven, and bake uncovered 20 minutes, or until fish easily flakes with a fork.

Serve with Sautéed New Potatoes with Rosemary and Brussels Sprouts in Garlic Butter.

• SAUTÉED SALMON WITH ORANGE AND DILL •

Dill lends a lightness to fish but you must use fresh to truly experience it. If you live in the proper climate, plant your own. But if you don't, many supermarkets carry fresh dill in the produce section. Feel free to substitute orange roughy fillets for the salmon.

PREP: 5 minutes   COOK: 25 minutes

INGREDIENTS
  2 teaspoons olive oil
  2 (4 - 6 ounce) salmon fillets, skin removed
  2-1/2 cups orange juice
  3 sprigs fresh dill weed

DIRECTIONS

1. Heat olive oil in a 10-inch skillet over medium heat. Add salmon fillets and pour orange juice over salmon. Arrange dill sprigs around the salmon. Cook, turning occasionally, for 15 minutes, or until fish is easily flaked with a fork. Remove salmon to a warm dish and cover loosely.

2. Reduce skillet heat to medium-low, and continue cooking the orange juice 10 minutes until slightly thickened, about 10 minutes. Pour over the salmon to serve.

Serve with Roasted Red Potatoes and Parmesan and Steamed Summer Squash.

• MEDITERRANEAN SALMON •

Extra virgin olive oil, balsamic vinegar, garlic and fresh basil are staples of Mediterranean Cuisine. Here they are combined to marinate the salmon fillets, producing a tart, yet fruity entrée.

PREP: 5 minutes   MARINATE: 10 minutes
COOK: 15 minutes

INGREDIENTS
    1/4 cup extra virgin olive oil
    2 tablespoons balsamic vinegar
    2 cloves garlic, pressed
    2 (4 – 6 ounce) salmon fillets
    2 teaspoons chopped fresh cilantro
    2 teaspoons chopped fresh basil
    1/2 teaspoon kosher salt

DIRECTIONS

1. Prepare outdoor grill or preheat broiler.

2. Combine the olive oil and balsamic vinegar in a small bowl.

3. Arrange salmon fillets in a shallow baking dish. Rub garlic onto the fillets then pour the vinegar and oil over them, turning once to coat. Season with cilantro, basil, and salt. Set aside to marinate for 10 minutes.

4. Grill or broil salmon about 6 inches from the heat source about 6 minutes per side until nicely browned and easily flaked with a fork. Brush occasionally with the sauce from the pan.

Serve with Buttered Noodles and Sautéed Broccoli with Garlic and Red Pepper.

• LEMON ROSEMARY SALMON •

Here the cleansing taste of fresh lemon is enhanced by the lemony-pine flavor of fresh rosemary.

PREP: 10 minutes   COOK: 20 minutes

INGREDIENTS
    1 lemon, thinly sliced
    4 sprigs fresh rosemary
    2 (4 – 6 ounce) salmon fillets, skin removed
    Kosher or sea salt to taste
    1 tablespoon extra virgin olive oil, or as needed

DIRECTIONS
1. Preheat oven to 400°.

2. Arrange half the lemon slices in a single layer in a lightly-oiled baking dish. Layer with 2 sprigs rosemary, and top with salmon fillets. Sprinkle salmon with salt, layer with remaining rosemary sprigs, and top with remaining lemon slices. Drizzle with olive oil.

3. Bake 15 - 20 minutes, or until fish is easily flaked with a fork.

Serve with Rice Pilaf with Wine and Tomatoes.

• BAKED SALMON WITH BELL PEPPER AND LEMON •

This is another *en papillote* dish, one baked in foil or parchment. The piquancy of the capers offers a nice contrast to the sweetness of the red peppers.

PREP: 5 minutes   MARINATE: 1 hour
COOK: 35 minutes

INGREDIENTS
    1/4 cup extra virgin olive oil
    2 cloves garlic, chopped
    3 tablespoons lemon juice
    1 pinch kosher salt
    2 (4 - 6 ounce) salmon fillets
    2 tablespoons capers, drained and rinsed
    1/2 red bell pepper, cut into 1/4-inch strips

DIRECTIONS
1. Combine the olive oil, garlic, lemon juice, and salt in a small baking dish. Pierce the salmon fillets on both sides with a fork, and place in the dish. Coat with the olive oil mixture, and marinate at least 1 hour in the refrigerator, turning at least once.

2. Preheat oven to 375°.

3. Place each salmon fillet on a large sheet of aluminum foil. Fold the foil around the fillets to form packets. Pour the marinade mixture over the fillets, and top with capers and red bell pepper strips. Tightly seal packets, and place in a baking dish.

4. Bake salmon 35 minutes.

Serve with Parmesan Noodles and Broccoli Amandine.

• BAKED SALMON WITH PINEAPPLE TOMATO SALSA •

I love the salsa in this recipe. You may use canned pineapple but the tomato and basil must be fresh.

PREP: 10 minutes   COOK: 40 minutes

INGREDIENTS
    2 tablespoons lime juice
    2 tablespoons extra virgin olive oil
    1 tablespoon soy sauce
    2 tablespoons chopped shallots
    1/2 teaspoon brown sugar
    1/4 cup diced pineapple
    1 large plum tomato, diced
    2 tablespoons chopped fresh basil
    Salt and pepper to taste
    2 (4 - 6 ounce) fillets salmon
    1/4 cup dry white wine or chicken broth
    Lemon pepper to taste

DIRECTIONS
1. Preheat oven to 375°.

2. Whisk together the lime juice, olive oil, soy sauce, shallots, and brown sugar in a small bowl. Stir in the pineapple, tomatoes, and basil. Season with salt and pepper to taste. Reserve salsa.

3. Place salmon in a small baking dish. Pour wine or chicken broth over the top, and sprinkle with lemon pepper.

4. Bake in a preheated oven until fish flakes easily with a fork, about 30 to 40 minutes. Top with reserved salsa and serve.

Serve with Steamed White Rice and Cuban Black Beans.

• BAKED ORANGE ROUGHY WITH HERB SAUCE •

This New Zealand fish has become increasingly popular in America over the past few years. Mild in taste and firm in flesh, orange roughy readily assimilates a variety of seasonings and sauces. This sherry-based herb sauce is particularly appealing to the palate.

PREP: 10 minutes   COOK: 40 minutes

INGREDIENTS
- 2 teaspoons unsalted butter
- 2 teaspoons all-purpose flour
- 2 tablespoons chicken broth
- 2 tablespoons sherry
- 1-1/2 teaspoons chopped fresh chives
- 1/8 teaspoon dried basil
- 1/8 teaspoon dried thyme
- 2 (4-6 ounce) orange roughy fillets
- 1/8 teaspoon kosher salt
- 1/8 teaspoon black pepper
- 1 tomato, peeled and sliced

DIRECTIONS
1. Preheat oven to 300°. Lightly butter a small baking dish.

2. Melt butter in a small saucepan over medium heat. Stir in flour and whisk until well-blended, about 5 minutes or more. Gradually add chicken broth and sherry, stirring constantly, until thick and bubbly. Stir in chives, basil, and thyme. Remove from heat, and set aside.

3. Place the orange roughy fillets in the baking dish and season with salt and pepper. Arrange tomato slices over the fish then pour the sauce over.

4. Bake 30 to 40 minutes until fish is easily flaked with a fork.

Serve with Rice with Pine Nuts and Raisins along with Sautéed Spinach and Garlic.

• SAUTÉED ORANGE ROUGHY WITH CITRUS SAUCE •

Citrus has always been an important option in the preparation of seafood. Here we combine three different juices to create a sweet and piquant essence.

PREP: 10 minutes   COOK: 10 minutes

INGREDIENTS
    2 (4-6 ounce) orange roughy fillets
    1/4 cup milk
    1/8 teaspoon kosher salt
    3 tablespoons all-purpose flour
    1-1/2 tablespoons olive oil, divided
    1-1/2 teaspoons minced garlic
    1-1/2 tablespoons fresh lime juice
    1 tablespoon lemon juice
    1-1/2 teaspoons orange juice
    2 teaspoons chopped fresh parsley
    1 tablespoon thinly sliced green onion
    2 teaspoons unsalted butter

DIRECTIONS
    1.   Soak fish in milk 10 minutes. Remove, sprinkle with salt and dredge in flour.

    2.   Heat 1 tablespoon oil in a 10-inch skillet over medium-high heat. Add fillets and cook until golden on one side, about 3 minutes. Cook second side until golden and cooked through, about 3 to 4 more minutes. Remove fish to a serving platter.

    3.   Wipe skillet clean. Reduce heat to low, add remaining oil and sauté garlic 30 seconds. Add lime juice, lemon juice, orange juice, parsley, and green onions. Add butter and swirl until just creamy. Pour sauce over fish and serve.

Serve with Rice Pilaf and Steamed Green Beans.

• BAKED ORANGE ROUGHY WITH TOMATOES • AND FRESH SPINACH

This recipe is also excellent with grouper fillets. Be sure to wash and dry the fresh spinach to remove any sand or grit before adding to the skillet.

PREP: 10 minutes   COOK: 30 minutes

INGREDIENTS
   2 (4 – 6 ounce) orange roughy fillets
   1 tablespoon olive oil
   1/2 cup finely chopped onion
   1 clove garlic, minced
   1 14.5-ounce can chopped tomatoes with juice
   1/4 cup dry white wine
   5 ounces fresh spinach, stems removed
   1 tablespoon chopped fresh dill, or 1-1/2 teaspoons dried
   1 tablespoon chopped fresh parsley
   1 tablespoon fresh lemon juice
   1/8 teaspoon white pepper

DIRECTIONS
   1.   Preheat oven to 400°.

   2.   Heat olive oil in a 10-inch skillet over medium-high heat. Add onion and sauté until soft and translucent, about 8 minutes. Add garlic and sauté 1 additional minute. Add the tomatoes and wine and cook for 8 minutes until slightly reduced. Add the spinach. Cover and cook for 3 to 5 minutes until spinach has wilted. Remove from heat and add the dill, parsley and lemon juice. Set aside.

   3.   Grease a small baking dish. Pour half the sauce into the dish then add the fillets. Sprinkle with pepper and pour remaining sauce over all. Cover and bake for 15 minutes or until fish flakes easily with a fork.

Serve with Rice Pilaf.

• GRILLED MARINATED SWORDFISH •

When I am at the market to buy salmon and I spy fresh swordfish resting on the ice, well, it is time to change the night's recipe.

PREP: 10 minutes   MARINATE: 1 hour
COOK: 12 minutes

INGREDIENTS
    2 cloves garlic, crushed
    3 tablespoons dry white wine
    2 tablespoons lemon juice
    1 tablespoon soy sauce
    1 tablespoon olive oil
    1/4 teaspoons dried thyme
    1/8 teaspoon kosher salt
    1/8 teaspoon freshly ground pepper
    10 to 12 ounce swordfish steak(s)
    1-1/2 teaspoons chopped fresh parsley
    2 slices lemon

DIRECTIONS
1. Combine the garlic, white wine, lemon juice, soy sauce, olive oil, thyme, salt, and pepper in a small baking dish. Place swordfish steaks into the marinade, and refrigerate for 1 hour, turning frequently.

2. Preheat an outdoor grill or indoor broiler for high heat.

3. Grill swordfish steak(s) for 5 to 6 minutes on each side. Garnish with parsley and lemon wedges.

Serve with Roasted Red Potatoes with Parmesan and Green Beans Niçoise.

• HERBED STUFFED SWORDFISH •

This is a unique way to prepare swordfish. Be sure to pound the fillets gently so they do not tear. This recipe also works well with orange roughy and red snapper fillets.

PREP: 15 minutes   COOK: 7 minutes

INGREDIENTS
   2 (4 – 6 ounce) swordfish fillets, 1/2 inch thick
   1/4 cup chopped fresh parsley, divided
   2 tablespoons plain dried bread crumbs
   1/4 teaspoon orange zest
   1/4 teaspoon oregano
   1/4 teaspoon rosemary
   1/2 teaspoon kosher salt, divided
   1/4 cup orange juice, divided
   1 tablespoon orange marmalade
   1 tablespoon red wine vinegar
   1 teaspoon extra virgin olive oil
   1/4 cup diced roasted red pepper (jarred is fine)
   1/2 small red onion, diced
   1 small rib celery, diced

DIRECTIONS
1.   Preheat oven to 400°.

2.   Place swordfish fillets between two pieces of waxed paper and pound to 1/4 inch thickness.

3.   Combine 2 tablespoons parsley with the bread crumbs, orange zest, oregano, rosemary and 1/4 teaspoon of the salt in a small bowl.

4.   Sprinkle fillets with 2 tablespoons orange juice and spoon parsley mixture over fillets. Roll fillets up neatly and place seam side down in a small greased baking dish. Cover with foil and bake for 7 minutes or until fillets are just opaque.

5.   Meanwhile, combine the remaining orange juice, marmalade, olive oil, red pepper, onion, celery, and remaining salt in a small saucepan. Warm over low heat.

6.   Place fish on plates and spoon sauce over all.

Serve with Brown Rice with Cashews and Maple Glazed Carrots.

Table for Two Tips:

Remove fish from the refrigerator 15-20 minutes before cooking to remove the chill.

If you are going to grill fish, make sure your grill is clean and oiled. Grab some paper towels and a pair of tongs. Dip the paper towels or kitchen towel in some vegetable oil and rub it onto the grill. You can also use cooking spray, just make sure that your grill is off or the spray could ignite and burn you.

For even easier grilling, purchase a grilling basket. It will keep the fish intact when turning and, if you keep it clean, will prevent the fish from sticking.

Another interesting method to keep fish from sticking to the grill – dip fish fillets, skin–side down, on a plate of kosher salt. The salt creates a barrier between the fillet and the grate. Simply brush the excess salt off before serving. This method works particularly well when you are grilling at a park where the grate may not be very clean.

Purchase a pair of tweezers and keep them in a kitchen drawer. They make an excellent tool to remove small bones from fish fillets.

Since fish cools quickly, preheat your plates and serve the fish right away.

• BROILED SWORDFISH WITH SPICY HONEY SAUCE •

One of the benefits of fish fillets is the incredibly small amount of time it takes to prepare them. Here we have a recipe that will be ready in just over 10 minutes.

PREP: 5 minutes   COOK: 6 minutes

INGREDIENTS
- 1/4 teaspoon lemon zest
- 2 tablespoons fresh lemon juice
- 2 tablespoons honey
- 1/2 teaspoon turmeric
- 1/2 teaspoon cumin
- 1/4 teaspoon ginger
- 1/4 teaspoon kosher salt
- 1/4 teaspoon hot sauce
- 2 (4 - 6 ounce) swordfish fillets
- 1/2 red bell pepper, finely diced
- 1 tablespoon chopped fresh parsley

DIRECTIONS

1. Preheat broiler to high.

2. In a small bowl combine the lemon zest, lemon juice, honey, turmeric, cumin, ginger, salt and hot sauce.

3. Place the fillets on a greased broiler rack and sprinkle with 1 tablespoon of the lemon-honey mixture. Broil 6 inches from heat, 3 minutes per side, until fish is just opaque.

4. Remove fish to plates. Stir the bell pepper and parsley into remaining lemon-honey mixture and spoon over fillets.

Serve with Garlic Smashed Potatoes and Green Beans with Sautéed Mushrooms.

• GRILLED TUNA STEAK •

It's a shame, but many tuna steaks are ruined due to over-cooking. Here is the key: when the steaks are cooked about 1/4" through, turn them over and continue to cook until the other 1/4" is cooked. Remove from the grill and let sit for a bit- they will continue to cook.

PREP: 5 minutes   MARINATE: 1 hour
COOK: 12 minutes

INGREDIENTS
   2 (4 - 6 ounce) tuna steaks, 1-inch thick
   2 tablespoons soy sauce
   1 tablespoon sherry
   1 tablespoon olive oil
   1 teaspoon lime juice
   1 small clove garlic, minced

DIRECTIONS
1. Combine the soy sauce, sherry, olive oil, lime juice, and garlic in a small bowl. Place tuna steaks in a shallow baking dish and pour the soy sauce mixture over the steaks. Cover, and refrigerate for at least one hour, turning frequently.

2. Preheat grill or broiler for high heat.

3. Place tuna steaks on grill, and discard remaining marinade. Grill for 3 to 6 minutes per side, or to desired doneness.

Serve with Orange Rice and Steamed Asparagus.

• TUNA NIÇOISE •

Niçoise refers to the cuisine found in and around the French Riviera city of Nice. This style of preparation includes tomatoes, black olives, garlic and anchovies. In this recipe, the stuffed green olives are substituted for the black olives and anchovy paste is substituted for anchovies.

PREP: 10 minutes   MARINATE: 15 minutes
COOK: 6 minutes

INGREDIENTS

- 2 (4–6 ounce) tuna steaks
- 1/4 cup olive oil plus one tablespoon, divided
- 1/4 teaspoon thyme
- 1/4 teaspoon rosemary
- 1 small clove garlic, crushed
- Salt and pepper to taste
- 2 teaspoons unsalted butter
- 1 tablespoon finely chopped scallions

- 2 teaspoons finely chopped stuffed olives
- 2 teaspoons finely chopped capers
- 1 tablespoon balsamic vinegar
- 1/2 teaspoon anchovy paste
- 1 tablespoon finely chopped parsley

DIRECTIONS

1. Combine 1 tablespoon olive oil, thyme, rosemary, garlic, salt, and pepper in a small bowl.

2. Place the tuna steaks in a small baking dish and pour olive oil mixture over all. Turn steaks, cover and let stand for 15 minutes.

3. Heat the butter in a 10-inch skillet over medium-high heat. Add the steaks and cook for 3 minutes. Turn and cook an additional 3 minutes.

4. Meanwhile, combine the onions, olives, capers, vinegar, and anchovy paste in another small bowl. Stir in the remaining olive oil and parsley.

5. Remove the tuna steaks to a serving dish and smooth half the sauce on top. Serve remaining sauce on the side.

Serve with Buttered Noodles and Steamed Green Beans and Walnuts.

• HERB MARINATED TUNA FILLETS •

This savory herb marinade also works well with mahi-mahi and grouper fillets.

PREP: 10 minutes   MARINATE: 1 to 2 hours
COOK: 10 minutes

INGREDIENTS
   3 tablespoons lime juice
   2 tablespoons white wine vinegar
   1 teaspoon kosher salt
   1/8 teaspoon freshly ground black pepper
   1/4 teaspoon ground ginger
   1/4 teaspoon dried basil
   1/4 teaspoon dried parsley
   1/8 teaspoon dried thyme
   1 teaspoon hot sauce
   1 pinch cayenne pepper
   3 tablespoons olive oil
   2 (4 – 6 ounce) tuna fillets

DIRECTIONS
   1.   Combine the first 11 ingredients in a small bowl.

   2.   Place the fish fillets in a small baking dish and pour the marinade over all. Turn, cover, and refrigerate for 1 to 2 hours.

   3.   Preheat broiler or an outdoor grill for high heat.

   4.   Place fish onto the grill or a broiling pan. Discard marinade. Grill or broil fish about 6 -8 minutes turning once, until the fish flakes easily with a fork.

Serve with Rice Pilaf and Carrots in Vermouth.

• GRAPEFRUIT MARINATED HALIBUT STEAKS •

This is a clean and refreshing way to prepare just about any fish steak. Feel free to experiment with different citrus juices for added variety.

PREP: 5 minutes   MARINATE: 1 – 2 hours
COOK: 20 minutes

INGREDIENTS
  1/4 cup grapefruit juice
  2 tablespoons olive oil
  1 teaspoon chopped fresh marjoram
  1/4 teaspoon kosher salt
  1/8 teaspoon ground black pepper
  2 (6 - 8-ounce) halibut steaks
  8 grapefruit sections (optional)
  2 sprigs fresh marjoram to garnish

DIRECTIONS
  1. Combine the grapefruit juice, olive oil, marjoram, salt, and pepper in a small bowl. Place steaks in a small baking dish and pour sauce over. Turn, cover and refrigerate 1 to 2 hours, turning frequently.

  2. Preheat grill or broiler.

  3. Remove fish and reserve marinade. Grill or broil steaks 5 – 6 minutes per side, brushing with reserved marinade, until steaks are barely opaque in thickest part.

  4. Remove steaks to a serving plate; scatter grapefruit sections around steaks. Garnish with sprigs of marjoram.

Serve with Boiled New Potatoes and Sautéed Garlic Broccoli.

• BAKED SNAPPER AND SHRIMP •

The red snapper, with its reddish-pink skin and red eyes, is one of the most impressive fish in the market display case. Once dangerously over-fished, new management techniques will hopefully insure that this magnificent fish will be available for generations to come.

PREP: 5 minutes   COOK: 40 minutes

INGREDIENTS
  1-1/2 tablespoons unsalted butter
  2-1/2 teaspoons all-purpose flour
  1/4 teaspoon kosher salt
  1/3 cup milk
  12 ounces red snapper fillets
  1/4 pound ounces cooked medium shrimp, peeled and deveined
  1-1/2 tablespoons grated Parmesan cheese

DIRECTIONS
  1. Preheat oven to 325°.

  2. Melt butter in a small saucepan, over medium-low heat. Whisk in flour and salt to make a paste and cook for 3 or 4 minutes. Gradually whisk in milk. Stirring constantly, cook until sauce is thick enough to coat the back of a spoon.

  3. Grease a small casserole dish and arrange the fillets and cover with shrimp. Pour white sauce over shrimp then sprinkle with grated cheese.

  4. Bake, uncovered, for 20 to 25 minutes until fish flakes easy with a fork.

Serve with Boiled New Potatoes and Green Beans Niçoise.

• BROILED GROUPER WITH CREAMY CRAB SAUCE •

Double this recipe for company. Trust me, they'll think you labored in the kitchen for hours using only the most exotic ingredients. Truth be told, you probably have most of these items on hand. So go ahead and make it. We'll keep the secret of its simplicity between us.

PREP: 5 minutes   COOK: 10 minutes

INGREDIENTS
1-1/2 tablespoons unsalted butter
1/2 cup heavy cream
1/4 teaspoon Dijon mustard
1 (6-ounce) can crabmeat, drained and flaked
1/4 teaspoon Cajun or Creole seasoning
Salt and pepper to taste
2 (6-ounce) grouper fillets
1 teaspoon olive oil
1 tablespoon lemon juice
1/4 teaspoon chopped fresh parsley
Salt and pepper to taste

DIRECTIONS
1. Preheat the oven broiler.

2. Melt butter with cream in a small saucepan over medium heat. Add the mustard and stir until thickened. Add the crab and season with Cajun seasoning, salt and pepper. Cook until heated through.

3. Place grouper in a small, greased baking dish, and rub with olive oil, lemon juice, and parsley. Season with salt and pepper.

4. Broil grouper about 4 minutes on each side, until easily flaked with a fork. Spoon the crab sauce over fish and serve.

Serve with Garlic Smashed Potatoes and Corn.

• SHRIMP SCAMPI •

"Scampi" is the plural for scampo, the Italian name for a small, lobster-like crustacean known as the Norway lobster. The lobster tails are traditionally prepared by sautéing them in a skillet with olive oil, garlic and white wine. When the Italians immigrated to America, they substituted shrimp for the scampi but kept both names. This dish has many variations, however, I believe this version is the simplest and best.

PREP: 10 minutes   COOK: 10 minutes

INGREDIENTS
    1 pound large shrimp, peeled and deveined
    1/4 cup unsalted butter or extra-virgin olive oil
    3 cloves garlic, crushed
    2 teaspoons minced parsley
    2 tablespoons dry white wine
    1 tablespoon lemon juice
    Salt and pepper, to taste
    Lemon slices to garnish (optional)
    Parsley sprigs to garnish

DIRECTIONS

1. Rinse shrimp and set aside.

2. Heat butter in 10-inch skillet over medium-low heat. Sauté garlic 1 - 2 minutes or until softened (do not brown).

3. Raise heat to medium-high and add shrimp. Sauté until pink and firm, about 1 to 2 minutes. Turn shrimp and add parsley. Sauté for 1 – 2 minutes more. Stir in white wine and lemon juice then season with salt and pepper. Sauté for 30 seconds.

4. Garnish with lemon slices and parsley sprigs.

Serve with Rice Pilaf and Broccoli with Garlic Butter.

• SHRIMP CREOLE •

Often confused with Cajun cuisine, Creole cooking is a bit more sophisticated in that it uses more butter and olive oil rather than the (sometimes) prodigious use of animal fat found in many Cajun recipes. And while both cuisines use green peppers, celery and onions as a base for many dishes, Creole cooks use more tomatoes, while Cajun cooks tend to use more spices. These two styles of cooking can, and should, be a part of the Table for Two kitchen.

PREP: 10 minutes   COOK: 30 minutes

INGREDIENTS
    3 tablespoons unsalted butter
    3 tablespoons all-purpose flour
    1 (14.5-ounce) can stewed tomatoes
    1 tablespoon tomato paste
    1/2 medium onion, chopped
    1/2 green bell pepper, chopped
    1 clove garlic, crushed
    1-1/2 tablespoons chopped fresh parsley
    1-1/2 cups chicken or shrimp broth
    1-1/2 teaspoons chili powder
    1 teaspoon kosher salt
    1/4 teaspoon ground black pepper
    1 pound medium shrimp, peeled and deveined

DIRECTIONS
1. Melt butter in a 10-inch skillet over medium heat. Stir in the flour and cook until browned, stirring constantly to make a brown roux, about 5 minutes.

2. Stir tomatoes, tomato paste, onion, green pepper, garlic and parsley, broth, salt and pepper into the roux. Bring sauce to a boil then reduce heat to medium-low. Simmer for 20 minutes. Add shrimp to mixture and cook until the shrimp turn pink and opaque.

Serve over Steamed White Rice.

• COCONUT SHRIMP •

Shrimp dishes are ubiquitous on Florida menus and Coconut Shrimp seems to be one of the most popular, particularly at beach eateries. Most coconut shrimp recipes insist that the shrimp be deep fried. But I'll leave that for the dives down by the docks. My favorite is one that sautés the shrimp in olive oil or butter. It's a little easier on the shrimp - and our arteries.

PREP: 10 minutes   MARINATE: 5 minutes
COOK: 5 minutes

INGREDIENTS
   1 pound extra-large shrimp, peeled and deveined, tails intact
   1 tablespoon lime juice
   1 egg, beaten
   1/2 cup all-purpose flour
   2/3 cup flaked coconut
   2 tablespoons olive oil or unsalted butter

DIRECTIONS
  1. Place the shrimp in a small bowl with the lime juice. Toss to coat and let sit for 5 minutes.

  2. Place the flour in a small bowl, the egg in another small bowl, and the coconut in another. Hold shrimp by tail and dredge in flour, shaking off excess flour. Dip in egg; allow excess to drip off. Roll shrimp in coconut, and place on a baking sheet lined with wax paper. Refrigerate for 30 minutes.

  3. Meanwhile, heat oil in a 10-inch skillet over medium-high heat. Add shrimp in batches: sauté, turning once, for 2 to 3 minutes, or until golden brown. Using tongs, remove shrimp to paper towels to drain. Serve warm with your favorite dipping sauce.

Serve with Rice with Pine Nuts and Raisins along with Simple Braised Carrots.

• CHIPOTLE SHRIMP •

Chipotle chilies are simply dried and smoked jalapeno peppers. This version packed in adobo sauce lends a sweet, smoky, and almost chocolate flavor to many dishes. Buy in small cans and transfer any leftover sauce to a small, covered plastic dish and refrigerate for other uses. Or better yet, freeze it then just cut off chunks as needed.

PREP: 10 minutes   COOK: 10 minutes

INGREDIENTS
  2 tablespoons unsalted butter
  1 clove garlic, minced
  2 tablespoons dry red wine
  2-1/4 teaspoons Worcestershire sauce
  1-1/2 teaspoons minced chipotle peppers in adobo sauce
  1/2 teaspoon kosher salt
  1 pound medium shrimp, peeled and deveined

DIRECTIONS
  Melt the butter in a 10-inch skillet over medium heat. Stir in the garlic, and sauté for 30 seconds. Stir in the red wine, Worcestershire sauce, chipotle peppers in adobo sauce and salt. Add shrimp, and sauté 1 – 2 minutes per side, or until opaque.

Serve over Steamed White Rice with Sautéed Glazed Tomatoes.

• CAJUN SHRIMP AND NEW POTATOES •

We talked about the difference between Cajun and Creole cuisines in a previous recipe. Here we see the use of the New Orleans' *'cooking trinity'* of onion, pepper and celery, no tomatoes and a good use of spice. And speaking of spice, feel free to use as much as your taste buds will allow.

PREP: 15 minutes   COOK: 25 minutes

INGREDIENTS
- 1 tablespoon olive oil
- 1/4 finely cup chopped onion
- 1/4 cup green pepper, chopped
- 2 tablespoons chopped celery
- 1 cup chicken broth
- 3 medium red potatoes, peeled and diced
- 1/2 teaspoon kosher salt
- 1 teaspoon Cajun or Creole seasoning
- 1/4 teaspoon freshly ground pepper
- 3/4 pound uncooked medium shrimp, peeled and deveined
- 2 tablespoons crumbled cooked bacon

DIRECTIONS

1. Heat the olive oil in a 10-inch skillet over medium-high heat. Add the onions and celery and sauté until the onions are soft and translucent, about 8 minutes. Add the chicken broth and bring to a boil.

2. Add potatoes, salt, Cajun seasoning and pepper. Reduce heat to medium and cook until potatoes are nearly tender, about 12 minutes.

3. Stir in the shrimp and bacon. Cover and cook for 3 – 5 minutes or until shrimp is pink and potatoes are tender.

Serve with Glazed Carrots.

• SHRIMP CURRY •

There are many versions of Shrimp Curry. This simple recipe embodies the rich and fragrant flavor of coastal South India, streamlined somewhat by the use of a good prepared curry powder.

PREP: 10 minutes   COOK: 25 minutes

INGREDIENTS
   2 tablespoons olive oil
   1 onion, chopped
   2 cloves garlic, crushed
   1 teaspoon finely grated ginger
   2 teaspoons cumin
   1-1/2 teaspoons turmeric
   1 teaspoon paprika
   1/2 teaspoon chili powder
   1 cup diced canned tomatoes
   1 cup unsweetened coconut milk
   1 teaspoon kosher salt
   16 large shrimp, peeled and deveined
   2 tablespoons chopped fresh cilantro
   2 tablespoons lemon juice

DIRECTIONS
   1.   Heat olive oil in a medium saucepan over medium heat. Add the onion and sauté for 10 minutes, until soft and translucent. Add garlic, ginger, cumin, turmeric, paprika and chili powder and sauté for 1 additional minute. Add the tomatoes, coconut milk, and salt; bring to the boil.

   2.   Reduce heat to medium-low and simmer, uncovered, for 8 minutes. Stir in shrimp and cilantro, cover, and simmer for another 4 minutes. Stir in the lemon juice.

Serve with Steamed White Rice.

• SHRIMP ÉTOUFÉE •

ÉTOUFÉE in French means 'smothered'. Funny. I could've sworn it meant 'delicious'. Try this dish and I think you'll agree with me.

PREP: 10 minutes   MARINATE: 5 minutes
COOK: 30 minutes

INGREDIENTS

1 pound shrimp, peeled and deveined   1/2 cup chopped onion
1/2 teaspoon basil   1 clove garlic, crushed
1/4 teaspoon thyme   1/2 cup sliced celery
1/4 teaspoon kosher salt   1/2 cup diced green
1/4 teaspoon ground black pepper   bell pepper
1/4 teaspoon crushed red pepper flakes   1/4 cup flour
4 tablespoons unsalted butter   1-1/2 cups chicken broth

DIRECTIONS

1. Combine the shrimp, basil, thyme, salt, pepper and red pepper flakes in a medium bowl; blend well. Cover and place in the refrigerator for 5 – 10 minutes.

2. Meanwhile, melt the butter in a medium saucepan or large skillet over medium heat. Add the onions, garlic, celery and green bell pepper and sauté until the vegetables are soft, about 8 - 10 minutes. And the flour and whisk to form a roux, about 3 - 5 minutes.

3. Stir in a small about of broth to make a paste, then slowly add the remainder, whisking constantly. Bring to a boil, then reduce heat to a simmer. (You may need to add more broth to create a gravy-like consistency.) Add the shrimp and simmer until the shrimp are cooked through, about 10 minutes. Add additional salt, pepper, and red pepper flakes to taste.

Serve with Steamed White Rice.

• GRILLED GARLIC SHRIMP •

Almost a grilled version of Shrimp Scampi (and some would call it thus). However, the addition of paprika, Italian seasoning and brown sugar adds complexity to an otherwise simple dish.

PREP: 10 minutes   MARINATE: 2 hours
COOK: 5 minutes

INGREDIENTS
- 1 teaspoon ground Hungarian paprika
- 1 tablespoon minced garlic
- 1 teaspoon Italian seasoning blend
- 1 tablespoon fresh lemon juice
- 2 tablespoons olive oil
- 1/4 teaspoon ground black pepper
- 1 teaspoon basil
- 1 tablespoon brown sugar, packed
- 1 pound large shrimp peeled and deveined

DIRECTIONS

1. Preheat an outdoor grill for medium-high heat or an indoor broiler.

2. Whisk the paprika, garlic, Italian seasoning, lemon juice, olive oil, pepper, basil, and brown sugar in a bowl. Stir in the shrimp, and toss to evenly coat with the marinade. Cover and refrigerate at least 2 hours, turning once.

3. Remove shrimp from marinade, drain excess, and discard marinade.

4. Place shrimp on grill and cook, turning once, until opaque, 2 - 3 minutes per side.

Serve with Rice Pilaf and Corn.

• THAI SPICED GRILLED SHRIMP •

This dish can be as spicy as you like. Add a little more hot sauce and chili paste for a bit more heat. But be careful - try this one first as detailed. You may find it to be more than hot enough.

PREP: 10 minutes   MARINATE: 2 hours
COOK: 5 minutes

INGREDIENTS
   3 tablespoons olive oil
   2 tablespoons sesame oil
   2 tablespoons chopped fresh parsley
   1 tablespoon hot sauce
   1 tablespoon minced garlic
   1-1/2 teaspoons ketchup
   1-1/2 teaspoons Asian chili paste
   1/2 teaspoon kosher salt
   1/2 teaspoon black pepper
   1-1/2 tablespoons lemon juice
   1 pound large shrimp, peeled and deveined
   6 wooden skewers, soaked in water

DIRECTIONS
   1.   Whisk together the olive oil, sesame oil, parsley, hot sauce, minced garlic, ketchup, chili paste, salt, pepper, and lemon juice in a small bowl.

   2.   Stir in the shrimp, and toss to evenly coat with the marinade. Cover and refrigerate at least 2 hours, turning once.

   3.   Preheat an outdoor grill for high heat or indoor broiler. Remove shrimp from marinade and thread onto skewers, piercing once near the tail and once near the head.

   4.   Lightly oil grill grate. Cook shrimp for 2 - 3 minutes per side until opaque, basting frequently with reserved marinade.

Serve with Orange Rice and Stir Fried Snow Peas.

• GARLIC BAKED SHRIMP •

This dish is so simple, yet so delicious. You can prepare it hours ahead and pop it in the oven at the last minute. I've made this for company and they've gone nuts over it. When I give them the recipe, they are stunned by its simplicity.

PREP: 10 minutes   COOK: 15 minutes

INGREDIENTS
   1 pound large shrimp, peeled and deveined
   3 tablespoons unsalted butter, melted
   2 cloves garlic, minced (or 1/4 teaspoon garlic powder)
   3 tablespoons seasoned breadcrumbs with Romano cheese
   1-1/2 tablespoons dry sherry (or dry white wine)
   1 tablespoon chopped fresh parsley

DIRECTIONS
   1.   Preheat the oven to 375°.

   2.   Place the shrimp in a small casserole dish and add the melted butter. Stir shrimp to coat well.

   3.   Add the remaining ingredients and stir to coat. May be refrigerated until ready to bake.

   4.   Place casserole dish in the oven and bake for 15 minutes (a little longer if the shrimp have been chilled.)

Serve with Basic Brown Rice and Corn.

• BAKED SHRIMP WITH FETA AND TOMATO •

When most of us think about using feta cheese, we usually think of salads. This recipe will change that. Feta cheese adds a wonderfully nuanced Greek touch to any dish. Feel free to experiment and use it in place of other cheeses in your recipes.

PREP: 15 minutes   COOK: 35 minutes

INGREDIENTS
   2 tablespoons unsalted butter
   1-1/2 teaspoons minced garlic
   1 pound large shrimp, peeled and deveined
   1/8 teaspoon crushed red pepper flakes
   1/2 teaspoon dried oregano
   Salt to taste
   2 tablespoons chopped fresh parsley
   6 tablespoons dry vermouth
   1/2 (14.5-ounce) can diced tomatoes
   2 ounces crumbled feta

DIRECTIONS

1. Preheat oven to 350°.

2. Melt the butter in a 10-inch skillet over medium-high heat. Add the garlic and sauté for 1 minute. Stir in the shrimp, red pepper flakes, and oregano. Cook until the shrimp are firm and opaque, about 5 minutes. Season with salt, stir in the chopped parsley then pour into a small casserole dish.

3. Pour vermouth into the skillet and simmer until reduced by half. Add chopped tomatoes and continue cooking until heated through. Spoon tomato mixture on top of the shrimp and sprinkle with crumbled feta cheese.

4. Bake until the cheese softens and turns golden brown, about 15 to 20 minutes.

Serve with Sautéed New Potatoes and Steamed Squash with Sun Dried Tomatoes.

• FROGMORE STEW •

This hearty stew hails from South Carolina's Low Country. No, there are no frogs in Frogmore Stew; it's named after the town that made it famous. If you are preparing this in a romantic setting, choose the alternate name: Land's End Stew. That sounds a little better, doesn't it?

PREP: 10 Minutes   COOK: 30 Minutes

INGREDIENTS
    8 cups water
    1/4 cup crab boil - Old Bay® Seasoning is fine
    1 lemon, halved
    1 bay leaf
    1 tablespoon kosher salt
    12 ounces new red potatoes
    12 ounces hot Italian sausage links, cut into 2 inch pieces (or substitute
        kielbasa for a milder version)
    4 ears corn - husked, cleaned and quartered
    1-1/4 pounds large fresh shrimp, unpeeled
    4 tablespoons unsalted butter (optional)
    Freshly ground black pepper

DIRECTIONS
1. Bring water and Old Bay® Seasoning to boil in a small Dutch oven or stockpot. Squeeze the lemons into the pot and add the peels, bay leaf and salt. Cook for five minutes.

2. Add potatoes and cook for 15 minutes. Add sausage and cook for 5 minutes more. Add corn and cook for another 5 minutes.

3. Remove from heat and stir in the shrimp. Cover and let stand for 5 minutes until shrimp are pink, about 5 minutes. Drain and stir in butter and serve with plenty of black pepper.

• SHRIMP AND SALMON CAKES •

A little more involved, but this is a nice change from traditional Maryland crab cakes (see below).

PREP: 20 minutes   COOK: 25 minutes
SET TIME: 15 minutes

INGREDIENTS
   6 ounces shrimp, peeled, deveined and minced
   1/2 cup finely chopped red bell pepper
   1-1/2 tablespoons olive oil, divided
   1 (6-ounce) can salmon, drained very well and flaked
   3/4 cup dry bread crumbs
   2-1/2 tablespoons grated Parmesan cheese
   3/4 teaspoon ground black pepper
   1/2 teaspoon dried basil
   1/4 teaspoon dried oregano
   1/4 teaspoon dried thyme
   1 tablespoon chopped fresh chives (or 1 teaspoon dried)
   1 fresh jalapeno pepper, seeded and chopped
   1 egg, well beaten
   1 (8-ounce) package cream cheese, softened

DIRECTIONS
   1.   Preheat oven to 450°.

   2.   Heat 1 tablespoon olive oil in a 10-inch skillet over medium-low heat, stir shrimp and red bell pepper until shrimp is partially cooked. Remove from heat, and set aside.

   3.   In a medium bowl, mix the bread crumbs, Parmesan cheese, black pepper, basil, oregano and thyme. Stir in shrimp, red bell pepper, salmon, remaining olive oil, chives and jalapeno pepper. Thoroughly blend eggs and cream cheese into the mixture.

   4.   Divide the mixture into about 4 patties (3/4 inch thick), and arrange on a lightly oiled baking sheet. Refrigerate for 15 minutes. Bake 20 to 25 minutes in the preheated oven, until lightly browned.

Serve with Roasted Red Potatoes and Creamed Spinach.

• SCALLOPS AND SHRIMP PROVENÇAL•

Provençal refers to food prepared in the style of Provence, a region in southeastern France. This style of cooking, with its good use of tomatoes, garlic, olive oil and onions has become more and more popular as studies reveal that the cuisines of the Mediterranean may be some of the healthiest.

PREP: 35 minutes   COOK: 50 minutes

INGREDIENTS
   1 tablespoon unsalted butter
   1/2 pound sea scallops, rinsed and drained
   1/2 small onion, finely chopped
   3 ounces mushrooms, thinly sliced
   1 clove garlic, minced
   1 medium tomato, peeled and chopped
   1-1/2 tablespoon dry white wine
   2-1/2 teaspoons ketchup
   1/8 teaspoon kosher salt
   1/8 teaspoon chopped dried tarragon
   1/8 teaspoon dried rosemary
   Pinch white pepper
   3 ounces small shrimp
   3/4 teaspoon white wine vinegar
   Chopped fresh parsley, for garnish

DIRECTIONS
   1. Preheat oven to 400°.

   2. Melt butter in a 10-inch skillet over medium-high heat. Without crowding, lightly brown scallops in batches. Remove scallops to two lightly buttered ramekins.

   3. Add onion and mushrooms to the skillet and sauté until the onion is soft and begins to brown, about 8 minutes. Stir in garlic, tomatoes, wine, ketchup, salt, tarragon, rosemary, and white pepper. Bring to a boil and cover, reduce heat to low and simmer 15 minutes. Uncover,

and cook until thick, about 3 minutes. Add shrimp and vinegar and cook for 1 – 2 minutes until shrimp is opaque.

4.   Spoon shrimp sauce evenly over scallops.

5.   Bake until sauce bubbles and begins to brown at the edges, about 10 minutes. Sprinkle parsley over the top and serve.

Serve with Boiled New Potatoes and Steamed Green Beans

Table for Two Tips:

The best way to defrost shrimp is in the refrigerator. Tossing frozen shrimp into a colander and running them under warm water is quicker, but that method will affect the texture and taste.

Not enough large shrimp in the fridge or freezer to create a dish? No problem. Simply cut the shrimp in half from head to tail to 'double' the amount. This is a good trick when unexpected company drops by.

If at all possible, cook all of your shrimp in the shell. They will taste much better – the flavor is in the shell. For ease in peeling, cut or slit the shells with scissors. Better yet, many markets now sell frozen shrimp that are pre-slit and de-veined. Of course, you may not want to do this with Shrimp Creole for company. But if it's just the two of you, and you don't mind making a mess, cook the shrimp-in-shell and go at it. As an aside, hardcore shrimp eaters don't even waste time removing the shell. They eat the wonderful crustacean shell and all, discarding the little tail fin along the way.

Don't toss out your shrimp shells. Save them and freeze. Sauté in a little olive oil until nice and pink then add to clam juice or fish stock and simmer. Strain before using to create an extra-rich stock.

Look for dry or unsoaked scallops. These have not been subjected to a phosphate solution that keeps them from releasing water after shucking. They will, however, release the water upon cooking, which will make sautéing a bit difficult. So stick with dry. When shopping, avoid scallops that look like a gelatinous mass in the seafood counter. They should be dry, separate and exhibit different color variations.

• SEA SCALLOPS IN CREAMY WHITE WINE SAUCE •

While I usually prefer bay scallops to the larger sea scallops in many dishes, grilling or broiling the smaller bay scallops is not really do-able. It's very important that you do not over-cook the scallops. They should be barely opaque. Remember, they will continue to cook after they are removed from the heat.

PREP: 5 minutes   COOK: 20 minutes

INGREDIENTS
    2 tablespoons dry white wine
    2 tablespoons white wine vinegar
    1 teaspoon minced shallots
    3 tablespoons heavy cream
    1/4 cup unsalted butter
    8 sea scallops
    1 teaspoon olive oil
    Salt and pepper to taste

DIRECTIONS
1.   Preheat broiler or grill to high.

2.   Combine white wine, wine vinegar and shallots in a small saucepan over medium-high heat. Cook until liquid is nearly evaporated, leaving about 1 tablespoon. Stir in heavy cream and reduce by half. Stir in butter 1 tablespoon at a time, allowing each to melt before adding the next. Remove from heat, cover and keep warm.

3.   Brush scallops with olive oil and sprinkle with salt and pepper. Place under preheated broiler for 2 minutes on each side, until scallops are opaque, with a bit of brown around the edges. Place a spoonful of sauce on each plate, and top with 4 scallops. Top with remaining sauce.

Serve with Rice with Wine and Tomatoes.

• GRILLED SEA SCALLOPS •

Is it possible to create an extraordinary main course in less than 15 minutes? Yes, and here it is: succulent sea scallops wrapped in rich prosciutto, then basted with butter and grilled.

PREP: 5 minutes   COOK: 10 minutes

INGREDIENTS
   1/2 pound sea scallops
   2 ounces prosciutto, thinly sliced
   2 tablespoons unsalted butter, melted
   Toothpicks, soaked in water

DIRECTIONS
   1.   Preheat grill or broiler to medium-high heat.

   2.   Wrap each scallop with a thin slice of prosciutto and secure with a toothpick.

   3.   Lightly oil grill grate. Arrange scallops on the grill and baste with butter. Cook for 3 minutes, turn, and baste with butter. Cook for another 3 - 5 minutes, or until opaque.

Serve with Boiled New Potatoes and Herb Baked Tomatoes.

• MARYLAND CRAB CAKES •

Everyone on Chesapeake Bay seems to have a different twist on this, but there seems to be two constants: Old Bay® Seasoning and lump crabmeat. Don't even attempt this with flaked. Placing the cakes in the fridge for 15 – 20 minutes will help keep them intact while you cook them.

PREP: 15 minutes   COOK: 15 - 20 minutes

INGREDIENTS
    1/2 cup crushed saltine crackers
    1/2 cup mayonnaise
    1/2 teaspoon prepared brown mustard
    2 tablespoons chopped onion
    2 tablespoons chopped celery
    1/2 teaspoon Old Bay® Seasoning
    1/2 pound lump crabmeat

DIRECTIONS
    1. Preheat broiler. Lightly grease a small baking sheet.

    2. Combine the crackers, mayonnaise, brown mustard, onion, celery, and Old Bay® Seasoning in a medium bowl. Gently stir in the crabmeat. Shape into 2 patties. Place on the baking sheet and refrigerate for 15 minutes.

    3. Broil crab cakes 8 to 10 minutes on each side, or until golden brown.

Serve with Sautéed New Potatoes with Rosemary and Lemon Pepper Peas.

• CRAB IMPERIAL •

This one is very rich. Sherry, cream, egg yolk, mayonnaise - well, you get the picture. I wouldn't eat it every day and neither should you, but for a special evening, it's hard to beat.

PREP: 20 minutes   COOK: 25 minutes

INGREDIENTS
   2/3 cup dry sherry
   2 teaspoons finely chopped shallots
   1/2 green bell pepper, finely chopped
   4 fresh mushrooms, thinly sliced
   1 tablespoon chopped pimento (jarred is fine)
   2 tablespoons heavy cream
   1 egg yolk
   3/4 teaspoon dry mustard
   12 ounces lump crabmeat
   2/3 cup mayonnaise
   1/3 cup Gruyere cheese, shredded

DIRECTIONS
   1. Preheat oven to 400°. Lightly butter 2 ramekins.

   2. Bring sherry to boil in a small saucepan over medium-high heat. Stir in shallots, green bell pepper, mushrooms and pimento. Cook, stirring occasionally, until only a small amount of liquid remains.

   3. In another small saucepan, whisk together heavy cream and egg yolk over low heat for about 3 minutes. Stir into the shallot mixture. Stir in dry mustard.

   4. Remove the mixture from heat and stir in the crab. Set aside to cool. (May be prepared ahead of time. Refrigerate if necessary).

   5. Stir the mayonnaise into the mixture then scoop into the ramekins. Top with Gruyere cheese and bake 10 minutes until lightly browned.

Serve with Orange Rice and Steamed Asparagus.

• BROILED LOBSTER TAIL •

Creating a lobster meal has become easier now that frozen lobster tail is available in many supermarkets, packed two to a package. This recipe works best with Florida or Caribbean rock lobster, although Maine lobster will do just fine. Be sure the tails are completely thawed.

PREP: 10 minutes   COOK: 15 minutes

INGREDIENTS
  2 fresh or frozen lobster tails (defrosted if frozen)
  2 tablespoons unsalted butter
  1 clove garlic, crushed
  2 tablespoons chopped fresh parsley
  1-1/2 teaspoons lemon juice
  1/2 teaspoon paprika
  Salt and pepper to taste

DIRECTIONS
1. Place the lobster, shell side down (on its back), on a cutting board. Cut the softer undershell straight up the middle with kitchen shears. If using rock lobster, pull out the vein that runs the length of the tail. Cut into the meat partially to butterfly it. Do not cut all the way through.

2. Melt the butter in a small skillet over medium heat. Add the garlic and sauté for 1 minute. Add the parsley and cook 1 – 2 minutes more. Do not let garlic brown.

3. Remove skillet from heat and stir in lemon juice, paprika, salt and pepper.

4. Place lobster tails in a small roasting dish and spoon butter sauce on top. Broil until lightly brown and the butter begins to bubble, about 2 – 3 minutes.

5. Turn off broiler and let lobster tails sit in oven for 6 – 8 minutes to finish cooking.

Serve with Garlic Smashed Potatoes and Green Beans Amandine.

Poultry

 # Chicken

If someone were to ask you to name an economical, carb-free, low-fat source of protein that was also versatile and readily available, you would likely answer "chicken". That's because chicken is America's most popular meat, surpassing beef, pork, and lamb in consumption per capita. We eat it fried, grilled, broiled, poached, sir-fried and barbequed. Chicken easily absorbs herbs, spices, and sauces, making it the equivalent of a culinary blank-slate. Since it's the primary source of animal protein through much the world, each culture has its own take on preparing this wonderful bird.

Chicken breasts, whether bone-in or boneless, are a boon to the table-for-two cook. They are readily available and easily stored, which is particularly beneficial if you purchase them on sale and freeze them. Skinless, boneless breasts work especially well in fast, low-fat cooking methods like grilling and sautéing. If your chicken breasts have skin, don't feel the need to remove it prior to cooking to prepare low-fat meals even though most of the fat is found in the skin. Simply rub the herbs, spices or sauce under the skin and cook, removing the skin before serving. This method will keep the meat more succulent and moist than one using skinless chicken; and the amount of added fat is fairly negligible.

While breasts may seem like the obvious choice when cooking for two, please don't forget about boneless and bone-in thighs and chicken leg quarters. Chicken thighs may be used in place of chicken breasts in a number of recipes, and leg quarters are ideal for grilling and barbequing. I've even included a recipe for roast chicken. Technically, it's not a recipe for two but there is something about this simply prepared, yet elegant dish that warrants inclusion. Besides, the leftovers are wonderful.

Whatever method of preparation you choose, you must handle raw chicken carefully. Make sure that the uncooked chicken does not come in contact with other foods, particularly those that will be served uncooked. Wash your cutting board and knife with hot soap and water after preparing the chicken. Better yet, buy two small cutting boards and use one for meat, the other for veggies. Oh, and don't forget to wash your hands thoroughly after handling chicken.

• SAUTÉED CHICKEN BREASTS •

This is as basic a chicken recipe as you will find. But don't let the simplicity fool you – the onion, garlic and rosemary, the cooking trifecta in some circles, will truly excite the palate. Double the recipe for company but don't tell them it only took minutes to prepare. Start cooking your rice before the chicken and you'll have a wonderful meal in less time than it would take you to order take-out chicken (and a lot healthier, too!)

PREP: 5 minutes   COOK: 15 minutes

INGREDIENTS
   2 boneless, skinless chicken breasts
   1 tablespoon olive oil
   1 small onion, thinly sliced
   1 garlic clove, minced
   1 teaspoon dried rosemary, chopped (or 2 teaspoons fresh)
   1/3 cup chicken broth
   Salt and pepper to taste

DIRECTIONS
   1.   Dry chicken breasts with paper towels.

   2.   Place a breast between two pieces of plastic or wax paper and pound it to 1/4" thickness. (Use the smooth side of a kitchen mallet or heavy can).

   3.   Heat olive oil in a 10-inch skillet over medium heat. Add the chicken breasts and sauté for 4 minutes.

   4.   Turn breasts and scatter the onion slices around the chicken and sauté for 4 additional minutes.

   5.   Add the garlic, rosemary and chicken broth. Cover and continue to cook for an additional 5 minutes, stirring occasionally, until onions are crisp and the chicken is cooked though.

Serve with Boiled New Potatoes and Maple Glazed Carrots.

• SAUTÉED CHICKEN BREASTS WITH HERBS, •
CITRUS AND ALMONDS

Now we take basic sautéed chicken breasts up a notch with the addition of Dijon mustard, lemon peel, orange marmalade and almonds.

PREP: 5 minutes   MARINATE: 1 hour
COOK: 15 minutes

INGREDIENTS
    2 bone-in chicken breasts
    2 tablespoons lemon juice
    2 tablespoons olive oil, divided
    1 tablespoon Dijon mustard
    1 clove garlic, minced
    Pinch dried rosemary
    2/3 cup chicken broth, divided
    1/4 teaspoon cornstarch
    1/4 teaspoon grated lemon peel
    2 tablespoons slivered almonds or chopped pecans or walnuts
    1 tablespoon orange marmalade or apricot preserves
    1 tablespoon unsalted butter
    Pinch of red pepper flakes or to taste
    Salt and pepper to taste
    1 tablespoon chopped fresh parsley
    2 Lemon slices to garnish

DIRECTIONS
1. Combine the lemon juice, olive oil, mustard, garlic and rosemary in a small bowl.

2. Place chicken breasts in a 1 quart plastic zip lock bag. Add marinade and coat thoroughly. Marinate in the refrigerator for 1 hour or all day.

3. Melt the butter in a 10-inch skillet over medium heat and add the chicken. Cook until lightly brown, about 4 minutes per side. Reserve marinade.

4. Remove chicken and put on a plate and cover with another plate to keep warm.

5. In a small bowl, dissolve cornstarch in 1 tablespoon of the chicken broth.

6. Strain reserved marinade into the skillet. Stir in the chicken broth and cornstarch mixture. Bring to a boil and stir until thickened and reduced by half, about 2 or 3 minutes.

7. Add marmalade, lemon peel, slivered almonds and butter. Stir in red pepper flakes. Season with salt and pepper to taste.

8. Return chicken breasts to the pan and heat. Sprinkle with parsley and serve with lemon slices on top.

Serve with Buttered Noodles and Steamed Brussels Spouts.

• CHICKEN CORDON BLEU •

Cordon Bleu is French for blue ribbon and originally referred to the blue sash worn by senior students at the Institut de Saint-Louis. The term now refers to anyone who has achieved a great distinction in his or her field, especially cooks. As a recipe title, cordon bleu traditionally referred to a dish made with thin slices of veal, interlaid with ham and cheese, then sautéed. For many with an aversion to the production of veal, or its cost, this dish has become the ultimate 'veal meal' substitute.

PREP: 5 minutes   COOK: 30 – 40 minutes

INGREDIENTS
   2 boneless, skinless chicken breasts
   3 tablespoons unsalted butter, divided
   1 tablespoon olive oil
   2 slices Swiss cheese
   2 slices prosciutto or smoked ham
   1/4 cup flour
   1/4 teaspoon paprika
   1/4 teaspoon kosher salt
   1/4 teaspoon freshly ground pepper
   1 egg beaten
   1/2 cup dried bread crumbs
   1/4 cup dry white wine
   2/3 cup chicken stock

DIRECTIONS
   1. Dry chicken breasts with paper towels.

   2. Place a breast between two pieces of plastic or wax paper and pound it to 1/4" thickness. (Use the smooth side of a kitchen mallet or a heavy can).

   3. Heat 2 tablespoons butter and the olive oil in a 10-inch skillet over medium heat.

4. Cover each breast with a slice of cheese and ham. Trim cheese and ham to fit. Roll up lengthwise and secure with a toothpick.

5. Mix the flour, paprika, salt and pepper together in a shallow dish. Dredge the chicken in the flour and shake off excess. Dip each breast in the egg then roll in the breadcrumbs.

6. Add chicken breasts to the skillet. Cook and turn until brown, about 10 minutes. Remove breasts and place on a plate and cover with another plate to keep warm.

7. Pour off the fat from the pan, add the wine and bring to a boil. Scrape any brown bits from the bottom of the pan and boil until the wine is reduced to about 2 tablespoons. Add the stock; continue to boil until reduced by half. Add remaining butter and swirl.

8. Season with additional salt and pepper to taste and pour over chicken.

Serve with Rice Pilaf and Caramelized Brussels Sprouts.

• CHICKEN PICCATA •

This is yet another dish that is traditionally prepared with veal. Some versions suggest capers as only an option, but I like the piquancy they bring to this dish so I use them regularly.

PREP: 10 minutes   COOK: 10 minutes

INGREDIENTS
   2 boneless, skinless chicken breasts
   1 tablespoon unsalted butter
   1 tablespoon olive oil
   1/4 cup flour
   1/2 teaspoon kosher salt
   1/8 teaspoon ground pepper
   2 tablespoons dry white wine, chicken broth, or water
   4 thin fresh lemon slices
   1-1/2 tablespoons lemon juice
   1-1/2 tablespoons capers, rinsed
   1-1/2 tablespoons chopped parsley or 1 tablespoon dried

DIRECTIONS
   1.   Dry chicken breasts with paper towels.

   2.   Place a breast between two pieces of plastic or wax paper and pound it to 1/4" thickness. Heat the butter and olive oil in a 10-inch skillet over medium heat.

   3.   Mix the flour, salt and pepper together in a shallow dish. Dredge the chicken in the flour and shake off excess.

   4.   Add chicken breasts to the skillet. Cook 4 minutes per side until meat is tender and opaque. Remove breasts and place on a plate and cover with another plate to keep warm.

   5.   Add wine to the skillet and cook for a minute or two. Scrape any browned bits from the bottom of the pan.

6. Add the lemon juice and bring to a boil. Return the breasts to the pan and place two lemon slices on each breast. Sprinkle with chopped parsley. Continue to cook for three minutes until the sauce thickens a bit.

7. Serve chicken sprinkled with capers and a sprig of parsley to garnish.

Serve with: Serve with Rice Pilaf and Grilled Tomatoes with Garlic.

Table for Two Tips

Whole Leg Quarters - A Cook's Bargain. I usually buy whole leg quarters at the market because they are readably available and inexpensive. Doing so allows me to create two different meals - one for legs and one for thighs. However, separating the two by cutting through the joint can be tricky. If you have a sharp meat cleaver, it's a bit easier. Just whack it. But if you want two neat cuts, you must cut through the joint. Miss it, and even your best knife may get stuck in the bone. But if you take the time to look, you'll notice the thin line of fat that runs right over the joint. Turn the leg quarter skin side down and cut through the line of fat and cleanly through the joint. It may take some practice, but once you get it down, you'll find yourself saving a good bit of money buying whole leg quarters and cutting them yourself.

Bone-in Boneless Chicken Breasts - Many recipes call for boneless, skinless chicken breasts but you will pay for the luxury of having someone else bone them and skin them. If you do not carefully monitor them, your chicken breasts may turn out to be dry and tough. Here is a wonderful technique that will guarantee succulent breasts every time - cook the chicken with the bone in, about 6 minutes per side or until the skin just bounces back when you poke it. Remove the chicken and, while still hot, cut and pull away the bone, then serve. Cooking with the bone in will render a juicier breast with increased flavor.

• CHICKEN MARSALA WITH MUSHROOMS•

The rich, smoky flavor of Marsala defines this classic Sicilian dish; one that is also traditionally prepared with veal. As in all of the wines used for cooking, Marsala does not have to be expensive. There are several reasonably priced domestic selections to choose from.

PREP: 10 minutes   COOK: 20 to 25 minutes

INGREDIENTS
    2 boneless, skinless chicken breasts
    2 tablespoons unsalted butter, divided
    1 tablespoon olive oil
    2 tablespoons flour
    1/4 teaspoon freshly ground pepper
    1/4 cup chopped onion (1 small onion)
    1 garlic clove, minced
    1/4 pound fresh mushrooms (or one 4 oz jar) sliced
    2 tablespoons dry Marsala wine
    1/2 cup beef stock
    Salt to taste

DIRECTIONS
1. Dry chicken breasts with paper towels

2. Place a breast between two pieces of plastic or wax paper and pound it to 1/4" thickness.

3. Heat the 1 tablespoon butter and the olive oil in a 10-inch skillet over medium heat.

4. Mix the flour, salt and pepper together in a shallow dish. Dredge the chicken in the flour and shake off excess.

5. Add chicken breasts to the skillet and cook 4 minutes per side until meat is tender, lightly brown and opaque. Remove breasts to a plate and cover with another plate to keep warm.

6. Add onion and sauté for 3 minutes. Add garlic and sauté for 1 minute.

7. Add mushrooms and sautè until lightly brown, 3 to 5 minutes

8. Return chicken breasts to the pan and pour the Marsala and stock over chicken. Bring to a boil, reduce the heat and simmer until sauce is reduced by about 1/3. Add remaining tablespoon of butter and swirl. Add additional salt and pepper to taste.

Serve with Buttered Noodles and Sautéed Spinach with Garlic.

Table for Two Tips

Skinning Chicken - Removing the skin from chicken pieces can be a messy job, particularly after one or two attempts as your fingers become slimy and you lose your grip. The solution? Grab the skin with a paper towel and gently pull the skin away, then toss the paper towel. No muss. No fuss.

Freezing Chicken Breasts - I stock up on boneless chicken breasts when they're on sale and freeze them. Here's one way to keep them neat and easily accessible: Wrap one or two breasts in a sandwich bag and lay them flat in a larger zip-lock freezer bag. Continue until the freezer bag is full. As an alternative, wrap breast in wax paper and place in the freezer bag. By doing so, you will avoid the ensuing glob that will result from tossing all the meat in together (and having to defrost the whole shebang when all you want is a breast or two).

• BAKED CHICKEN WITH MUSHROOMS AND SPINACH •

PREP: 10 minutes   COOK: 45 minutes

INGREDIENTS

2 boneless, skinless chicken breasts   2 slices provolone cheese
1 egg, beaten   1/4 cup chopped onion
1/2 cup bread crumbs   1/4 cup dry white wine
1/2 (10-ounce) package frozen spinach   1/4 lb mushrooms, sliced
1/4 teaspoon Italian seasoning   (or 4 oz. jar)
1/4 teaspoon nutmeg   1 garlic clove, minced
1 tablespoon unsalted butter or olive oil

DIRECTIONS

1. Preheat oven to 350°. Lightly butter a small baking dish.

2. Dry chicken breasts with paper towel

3. Beat the egg in a shallow bowl. Combine the bread crumbs and Italian seasoning in a shallow dish. Dip each breast in the egg and then dredge in the bread crumb mixture. Shake off excess and place chicken in baking dish.

4. Squeeze excess moisture from the defrosted spinach.

5. Melt butter in a medium skillet over medium heat and add the onions. Sauté for 8 minutes until they begin to soften and turn translucent. Add mushrooms and garlic. Sauté an additional 3 – 5 minutes until mushrooms soften and begin to lose their juice. Stir in spinach and nutmeg and cook until heated through.

6. Spread half of the spinach mixture on each breast and top with a slice of provolone cheese.

7. Pour wine around chicken and bake, uncovered, for 30 minutes until cheese is melted and the chicken is tender.

8. Spoon sauce over chicken and serve.

Serve with Rice Pilaf.

• CHICKEN PARMESAN WITH TOMATO SAUCE •

This classic dish finds its way from the neighborhood trattoria to your kitchen. The key is to not over-cook the chicken – it must remain tender and moist.

PREP: 10 minutes   COOK: 25 minutes

INGREDIENTS
   2 boneless, skinless chicken breasts
   1 tablespoon olive oil
   1/2 cup dry seasoned bread crumbs
   1/4 cup grated Parmesan cheese
   1 egg, beaten
   1 (8-ounce) can seasoned tomato sauce
   4 thin slices mozzarella or 2/3 cup shredded

DIRECTIONS
1.   Preheat oven to 350°.

2.   Dry chicken breasts with paper towels.

3.   Heat the olive oil in a 10-inch skillet over medium heat.

4.   Combine breadcrumbs and Parmesan cheese in a shallow dish. Place egg in a shallow bowl. Dip chicken in the egg then dredge in the breadcrumb/cheese mixture.

5.   Shake off excess and add chicken breasts to the skillet. Cook 4 minutes per side until lightly brown.

6.   Remove breasts and place in a baking dish. Pour tomato sauce over chicken and top with mozzarella cheese. Bake for 15 minutes or until cheese is melted and bubbling.

Serve with your choice of pasta and hot, crusty Italian bread.

• CHICKEN BREASTS WITH RED PEPPER SAUCE •

I love the taste of sweet, red bell peppers with their mild and incredibly juicy flesh. If you like to use a lot of red bell peppers, consider purchasing them at your local farmer's market. Although they may not have that pristine shape and appearance of those found in the supermarket, they'll be just as delicious and a whole lot cheaper. Pick up a few extra to chop and freeze, then add to recipes and sauces that do not require crisp, sautéed peppers.

PREP: 5 minutes   COOK: 35 – 40 minutes

INGREDIENTS
    2 boneless, skinless chicken breasts
    1 medium tomato, peeled and chopped
    1 small onion chopped
    1 small red pepper chopped
    1-1/2 teaspoons chopped fresh parsley or 1/2 teaspoon dried
    1-1/2 tablespoons chopped fresh basil or 1/2 teaspoon dried
    1/2 teaspoon kosher salt
    1/8 teaspoon dried thyme
    1/8 teaspoon hot pepper sauce (or more to taste)
    1/8 teaspoon ground pepper
    1 tablespoon unsalted butter
    1/4 cup white wine

DIRECTIONS
1. Dry chicken breasts with paper towels

2. Place a breast between two pieces of plastic or wax paper and pound it to 1/4" thickness.

3. Combine tomatoes, onion, red pepper, parsley, basil, salt, thyme, hot pepper sauce and pepper in a small or medium size saucepan. Bring to a boil; reduce heat and simmer, uncovered, for 20 minutes. Pour into a blender and puree until smooth. Return to the saucepan, cover and keep warm over very low heat.

4.   Melt the butter in a 10-inch skillet over medium heat. Add chicken breasts and cook until lightly brown, 4 minutes per side. Add wine and reduce heat. Simmer, turning breasts, for 10 minutes.

5.   Spoon the red pepper sauce onto plates and place the chicken breasts on top. Drizzle wine sauce over chicken and serve.

Serve with Roasted Red Potatoes and Steamed Green Beans.

• CHICKEN BREASTS WITH SPICY APRICOT SAUCE •

I'm very fond of chicken with fruit and this simple recipe is one of my favorites. For a nice change of pace, feel free to substitute orange marmalade for a bit more sweetness.

PREP: 5 minutes   COOK: 45 minutes

INGREDIENTS
    2 bone-in skinless chicken breasts
    1 tablespoon olive oil
    2/3 cup chicken broth
    1/4 cup apricot preserves
    1-1/2 teaspoons chili sauce
    1 teaspoon Dijon mustard
    Salt and pepper to taste

DIRECTIONS
1. Heat olive oil in a 10-inch skillet over medium-high heat. Add chicken and cook, turning until browned, 5 – 7 minutes per side.

2. Remove chicken to a plate and pour off fat. Add the broth and return chicken to the pan. Reduce heat, cover, and simmer for 25 – 30 minutes until chicken is very tender.

3. Remove chicken to a plate and cover with another plate to keep warm.

4. Combine the apricot preserves, chili sauce, and mustard in a small bowl. Add mixture to the liquid in the pan and bring to a boil, stirring constantly with a whisk. Season with salt and pepper to taste and pour over chicken to serve.

Serve with Brown Rice Pilaf and Steamed Broccoli.

• CHICKEN BREASTS WITH LIME BUTTER •

There's something about the taste of lime that adds a pleasant twist to simple chicken and fish dishes. Fresh is ideal, but we use so much I keep a bottle of Nellie and Joe's Key Lime Juice® in my refrigerator and it goes quickly. We even have a bottle of homemade Old Sour on the counter and use it liberally on vegetables, meats and fish when we want to brighten things up. Here the tangy taste of lime is combined with butter, chives and dill to make a delightfully cleansing sauce. *Note: The Lime Butter Sauce is also great on sautéed or grilled fish fillets.*

PREP: 5 minutes   COOK: 15 – 20 minutes

INGREDIENTS
    2 boneless, skinless chicken breasts
    Salt and pepper to taste
    1 tablespoon olive oil
    1 tablespoon lime juice
    2 tablespoons unsalted butter
    1 teaspoon minced chives
    1/2 teaspoon fresh dill or a pinch of dried dill

DIRECTIONS

1. Season chicken breasts with salt and pepper.

2. Heat olive oil in a 10-inch skillet over medium heat. And chicken and sauté 4 minutes on each side until lightly brown. Reduce heat to low and cover. Cook chicken for an additional 8 – 10 minutes until tender and opaque. Remove chicken and place on a plate, cover with another plate to keep warm.

3. Pour fat from skillet and wipe with a paper towel. Return pan to low heat and add lime juice. Cook until it begins to bubble. Add butter and stir until sauce thickens. Stir in chives and dill. Season with additional salt and pepper to taste and spoon over chicken.

Serve with Rice Pilaf and Braised Carrots.

• SAUTÉED CHICKEN WITH TARRAGON CREAM SAUCE •

I was almost tempted to call this Sautéed Chicken with Dragon-Wort Cream Sauce, Dragon-Wort being the alternate name for tarragon. But I figured no one would make it, let alone eat it. So if it's okay with you, we'll stick with tarragon.

PREP: 5 Minutes   COOK: 20 Minutes

INGREDIENTS
    2 boneless, skinless chicken breasts
    1 tablespoon unsalted butter or olive oil
    2/3 cup dry white wine or dry vermouth (I prefer the vermouth)
    1 teaspoon Dijon mustard
    1/2 tablespoon chopped fresh tarragon or 1/2 teaspoon dried
    1/4 teaspoon kosher salt
    Ground pepper to taste
    2/3 cup heavy cream

DIRECTIONS
1. Melt butter in a 10-inch skillet over medium-high heat. Add chicken breasts and cook 4 minutes per side until lightly brown. Remove breasts to a plate and cover with another plate to keep warm.

2. Add wine to the skillet and bring to a boil. Scrape up any brown bits from the bottom of the pan. Stir in mustard, tarragon, salt, and pepper. Add the cream and bring to a boil, whisking until the sauce thickens, 3 – 4 minutes.

3. Lower heat to medium, return chicken breasts to the skillet and turn to coat with the sauce. Simmer for 8 – 10 minutes until chicken is tender yet cooked through. Remove chicken to serving plate and spoon sauce over.

Serve with Rice and Peas.

• CHICKEN BREASTS WITH DIJON MUSTARD •
CREAM SAUCE

As noted earlier, one of the benefits of chicken is its ability to act as a blank canvas for any number of sauces. The Dijon Mustard Sauce in this recipe transforms this relatively bland piece of meat into a delectable entrée. This sauce is also a great addition to any white fish fillet.

PREP: 5 minutes   COOK: 15 minutes

INGREDIENTS
    2 boneless, skinless chicken breasts
    1/4 cup dry white wine
    1/4 pound mushrooms sliced (or 4 ounce jar)
    1 shallot (or 1 tsp minced onion)
    1 clove garlic, minced or pressed
    1/4 cup heavy cream
    1-1/2 teaspoons Dijon mustard
    1-1/2 tablespoons capers
    1-1/2 tablespoon fresh dill or 1/4 teaspoon dried
    Salt and pepper to taste

DIRECTIONS
1. Place chicken breasts in a small saucepan and cover with cold water. Bring to a simmer over medium-low heat for 10 – 15 minutes until chicken is opaque but moist. Skim any fat that floats to the top of the water.

2. While chicken is poaching, combine wine, mushrooms, shallots and garlic in a small skillet. Cook over medium-high heat until mushrooms are tender and the sauce reduces by about half.

3. In a small bowl, whisk together the cream and mustard then stir into the wine sauce. Add the capers and dill. Season with salt and pepper to taste.

4. Remove chicken breasts to a serving plate and pour sauce over the chicken.

Serve with Rice Pilaf and Peas and Pearl Onions.

• CHICKEN VERONIQUE •
(Chicken with Grapes)

I already mentioned how fond I am of chicken and fruit recipes. Hopefully, after trying one or two, you'll feel the same. Here's my version of the classic French Chicken Veronique.

PREP: 5 minutes   COOK: 15 minutes

INGREDIENTS
  2 boneless, skinless chicken breasts
  1 tablespoon unsalted butter or olive oil
  2 small shallots, minced
  1/4 cup dry white wine
  1/2 cup heavy cream
  1/4 pound seedless green grapes, halved (about 3/4 cup)
  Salt and pepper to taste

DIRECTIONS
1. Dry chicken breasts with paper towels.

2. Heat butter or olive oil in a 10-inch skillet over medium-high heat. Add chicken breasts and sauté 4 minutes per side until lightly brown. Remove breasts to a plate and cover with another plate to keep warm.

3. Add shallots and stir briefly. Add wine and bring to a boil, scraping any brown bits from the bottom. Stir in cream and bring to a boil until sauce thickens, about 3 – 5 minutes. Add chicken breasts and grapes and heat through. Serve breasts with sauce over top.

Serve with Rice Pilaf or Buttered Noodles with Nutmeg.

• CHICKEN AND MUSHROOMS FLORENTINE •

Florentine dishes are prepared in the style of Florence, Italy, where chicken, fish or eggs are presented on a bed of greens and sprinkled with cheese or a cheese sauce. Poaching the chicken before a brief run under the broiler will keep the chicken plump and juicy. Be sure to squeeze all of the moisture from the defrosted spinach to keep this dish from becoming too watery.

PREP: 5 minutes   COOK: 25 – 30 minutes

INGREDIENTS
  2 boneless, skinless chicken breasts
  1 small onion, quartered
  1/2 cup white wine
  1/2 cup chicken broth
  1 tablespoon unsalted butter
  1 cup sliced mushrooms
  1 (10-ounce) package frozen spinach, thawed
  1/4 teaspoon ground nutmeg
  1/4 teaspoon kosher salt
  1/8 teaspoon freshly ground pepper, or more to taste
  1 tablespoon grated Parmesan cheese

DIRECTIONS
1. Combine chicken, onion, wine, and broth in a small saucepan. Cover and bring to a boil. Reduce heat to medium-low and simmer until chicken is just opaque, about 15 minutes.

2. While chicken is poaching, melt butter in a small skillet over medium heat. Add mushrooms and sauté until they begin to lose their juice, about 5 minutes.

3. Preheat broiler. Squeeze moisture out of spinach and spread out in an even layer in a lightly buttered small baking dish. Sprinkle spinach with nutmeg, salt and pepper. Place chicken breasts on top of spinach. Spoon mushrooms over chicken breasts and sprinkle with cheese. Broil for 1 or 2 minutes until cheese is melted and bubbly.

Serve with Boiled New Potatoes.

• CHICKEN WITH BLACK CHERRY SAUCE •

Did I mention how fond I am of chicken and fruit? Thought so. Here's another favorite.

PREP: 5 minutes   COOK: 40 minutes

INGREDIENTS
    2 boneless, skinless chicken breasts
    1 tablespoon unsalted butter or olive oil
    1 cup black cherries, canned or frozen, sugar-free
    1-1/2 teaspoons Worcestershire sauce
    1/2 teaspoon brown sugar
    1 clove garlic, minced or pressed
    1 teaspoon dry sherry
    1/4 cup finely chopped onion
    1/4 cup raisins
    1 teaspoon cornstarch dissolved in 1-1/2 tablespoons cold water

DIRECTIONS
1.   Preheat oven to 350°.

2.   Melt butter in a 10-inch skillet over medium-high heat. Add chicken breasts and sauté until nicely brown, about 4 minute per side.

3.   Place chicken in an small buttered baking dish

4.   Meanwhile, place half the cherries, Worcestershire sauce, brown sugar garlic and sherry in a blender and puree until smooth.

5.   Pour pureed cherries in a small saucepan and add onions, raisins and cornstarch mixture. Cook, stirring, over medium-high heat until thickened.

6.   Pour cherry sauce over chicken, add remaining cherries and bake for 30 minutes.

Serve with Rice Pilaf and Steamed Peas.

• SAUTÉED CHICKEN WITH SOY SAUCE AND LEMON •

Since the seasonings are added to the dish after cooking the chicken, you may wish to remove the skin from the chicken legs and thighs before cooking for a lower fat version of this entrée.

PREP: 10 Minutes   COOK: 35 Minutes

INGREDIENTS
    1 tablespoon olive oil
    2 chicken legs and 2 thighs
    1 clove garlic, minced
    1-1/2 teaspoons lemon zest
    Pinch of cayenne pepper, to taste
    1 tablespoon soy sauce
    1/2 teaspoon sugar
    1/4 cup dry white wine
    1-1/2 teaspoons lemon juice

DIRECTIONS
    1. Heat oil in a 10-inch skillet over medium-high heat. Add chicken and brown on one side, about 5 minutes. Turn and brown on the other side, an additional 5 minutes.

    2. Remove chicken and reduce heat to medium. Add the garlic and sauté for 1 minute. Stir in the lemon zest, cayenne, soy sauce, sugar and wine. Return chicken to the skillet and turn in the sauce. Cover and reduce heat to medium-low and simmer, turning once or twice, until the chicken is cooked through, about 20 – 30 minutes.

    3. Remove chicken to a serving plate and add lemon juice to the sauce. Spoon sauce over chicken and serve.

Serve over White Rice along with Stir Fried Snow Peas.

• SAUTÉED CHICKEN IN RED WINE SAUCE •

This is my version of the famous Chicken Coq au Vin. Be sure to use a fruity red wine, like hearty burgundy. Add 2 tablespoons of brandy, if you have it on hand, to add a little more depth.

PREP: 10 Minutes   COOK: 35 Minutes

INGREDIENTS

2 chicken legs and 2 chicken thighs   1 bay leaf
Salt and pepper to taste   1 tablespoon unsalted butter
1/4 cup all-purpose flour   1 tablespoon chopped parsley
2 tablespoons olive oil
1 cup sliced mushrooms
8 - 10 small white onions peeled, frozen is fine
1 clove garlic, chopped
3/4 cup burgundy wine
1/4 teaspoon thyme

DIRECTIONS

1. Season chicken pieces with salt and pepper to taste. Place flour in a bowl or in a plastic bag. Dredge chicken pieces in flour and shake off the excess.

2. Heat oil in heavy skillet large enough to hold chicken pieces in one layer over medium-high heat. Add chicken pieces, mushrooms, onions, and garlic and cook until chicken is nicely browned, about 5 minutes. Turn and continue cooking an additional 5 minutes.

3. Pour fat from skillet and add the wine, thyme, and bay leaf. Cover and reduce heat to medium-low and simmer, turning once or twice, until the chicken is cooked through, about 20 – 30 minutes.

4. Transfer chicken, mushrooms and onions to a serving dish. Discard the bay leaf and reduce wine sauce over high heat, about 1 minute. Remove from heat, stir in butter and pour over chicken. Garnish with parsley and serve.

Serve with Roasted Red Potatoes and Steamed Asparagus.

• CHICKEN WITH 40 CLOVES OF GARLIC •

It seems everyone is a little hesitant the first time they prepare this dish. 40 cloves of garlic? Isn't that a bit much? It seems so on the surface, but you'll be surprised at how mild the garlic becomes after an hour of cooking. Of course, for the Table for Two version we will not be using 40 cloves. But I bet you'll increase the amount once you've tried this dish.

PREP: 10 Minutes   COOK: 1 Hour

INGREDIENTS
   2 chicken legs and 2 thighs
   1 tablespoon extra virgin olive oil
   1 head of garlic, separated but unpeeled
   1/4 cup chopped fresh parsley
   Salt and pepper to taste
   1/4 teaspoon allspice (or cinnamon)
   1/3 cup dry white wine or chicken broth

DIRECTIONS
   1.   Heat the olive oil in a medium Dutch oven medium heat. Add chicken and cook, turning, until golden brown, about 5 – 10 minutes.

   2.   Add garlic, parsley, salt, pepper and allspice and sauté for 1 minute. Pour the wine over and toss.

   3.   Bring mixture to a boil over medium-high heat. Cover, reduce heat to low and simmer, undisturbed, until chicken and garlic are tender, about 1 hour.

   4.   Transfer to a serving plate and serve. Squeeze the garlic cloves and spread over warm and crusty French bread.

Serve with Roasted Red Potatoes and Lemon Pepper Peas.

• SAUTÉED CHICKEN WITH BROCCOLI AND POTATOES •

This is a delicious and simple one-dish meal. Feel free to use asparagus, green beans or sliced carrots in place of the broccoli. Just be sure to adjust cooking time depending on the thickness of the vegetables to insure they are crisp-tender and not mushy.

PREP: 10 Minutes   COOK: 35 Minutes

INGREDIENTS
  1/2 pound small red potatoes
  1 tablespoon flour
  1/4 teaspoon Kosher salt, or to taste
  1/4 teaspoon freshly ground pepper, or to taste
  2 bone-in chicken breasts
  1 tablespoon olive oil
  4 cloves garlic, peeled
  1/4 teaspoon dried rosemary
  Pinch red pepper flakes
  2 tablespoons dry white wine
  3/4 cup chicken broth
  Salt and pepper to taste
  1-1/2 cups fresh broccoli florets

DIRECTIONS

1. Cook the potatoes in boiling water to blanch. About 5 minutes. Drain and set aside.

2. Mix the flour, salt and pepper on a plate and dredge chicken to coat. Shake off excess and set aside.

3. Heat olive oil in a 10-inch skillet over medium-low heat. Add the garlic, rosemary, and red pepper. Sauté until garlic is golden, about 4 minutes. Increase heat to medium-high, add chicken and cook until golden brown, about 3 minutes per side.

4. Add wine to the skillet and cook for 1 minute. Add broth, potatoes, salt and pepper to taste. Reduce heat, cover and simmer until chicken is nearly cooked through, about 18 minutes. Add the broccoli florets and cook, uncovered, about 3 minutes longer or until chicken is cooked through.

• BAKED CHICKEN BREASTS WITH HERBS •

This dish is very close to a full-fledged roast chicken. It's important that you use bone-in chicken with skin to insure a melt-in-your mouth breast. For those of you on a low fat diet, simply remove the skin before serving.

PREP: 15 Minutes   COOK: 45 Minutes

INGREDIENTS
  2 bone-in chicken breasts (with skin)
  2 tablespoons olive oil
  2 teaspoons minced onion
  1 clove garlic, crushed
  1/2 teaspoon dried thyme
  1/4 teaspoon dried rosemary, crushed
  1/8 teaspoon dried marjoram
  1/8 teaspoon ground sage
  1/8 teaspoon cayenne pepper
  1/4 teaspoon kosher salt
  1/4 teaspoon ground black pepper
  2 teaspoons chopped fresh parsley or 1 teaspoon dried

DIRECTIONS
  1. Preheat oven to 425 °.

  2. Combine the olive oil, onion, garlic, thyme, rosemary, marjoram, sage, cayenne, salt and pepper in a 1 quart plastic bag.

  3. Add the chicken breasts and shake to coat lightly. Marinate in the refrigerator for at least one hour or all day.

  4. Place chicken skin side up in a shallow baking dish along with the marinade. Roast, basting occasionally, for about 35 to 45 minutes until juices run clear when the chicken is pricked.

  5. Remove chicken to a warm platter, spoon pan juices over chicken and sprinkle with fresh parsley.

Serve with Garlic Smashed Potatoes and Orange Glazed Carrots.

• BAKED MEDITERRANEAN CHICKEN •

This is a lovely and simple dish. If you'd like to have less fat in your diet, you may remove the chicken skin before coating with the spice mixture. Or better yet, gently lift the chicken skin and rub the spice mixture under it, then remove the skin before serving.

PREP: 10 minutes   COOK: 50 minutes

INGREDIENTS
    3 tablespoons lemon juice
    1 teaspoon lemon zest
    1-1/2 teaspoons dried oregano
    2 cloves garlic, minced
    2 teaspoons olive oil
    1/8 teaspoon kosher salt
    1/8 teaspoon ground black pepper
    2 chicken legs and two chicken thighs (skinned if desired)

DIRECTONS
    1.   Preheat oven to 425°.

    2.   Combine the lemon juice, lemon zest, oregano, garlic, oil, salt and pepper in a small bowl. Add mixture to a buttered baking dish.

    3.   Add chicken pieces and toss to coat. Cover dish and bake for 20 minutes. Turn and baste chicken.

    4.   Reduce heat to 400° and bake uncovered for about 30 more minutes, basting every 10 minutes. Serve chicken with pan juices.

Serve with Roasted Red Potatoes (may be roasted in oven with the chicken) and Carrots in Vermouth.

• BAKED CHICKEN MILANO •

I like this one-dish meal because once it's in the oven, you can snuggle up to a loved one while nibbling Italian cheese and sipping a fine red wine. Simply add a tossed salad and warm Italian bread for a complete meal.

PREP: 15 Minutes   COOK: 1 Hour and 15 minutes

INGREDIENTS
  2 baking potatoes, cut into wedges
  Salt to taste
  1 clove garlic, minced
  1 red bell pepper, sliced
  1 (14.5-ounce) can stewed tomatoes
  1/2 pound sweet or hot Italian sausages, cut into two-inch slices
  2 chicken legs and 2 thighs
  Salt and pepper to taste
  1 tablespoon olive oil

DIRECTIONS

1. Preheat oven to 350°.

2. Place potatoes in a medium roasting pan and sprinkle with salt and garlic. Layer the pepper slices, tomatoes and sausages over the potatoes. Arrange the chicken pieces on top.

3. Brush chicken with the olive oil and season with salt and pepper to taste. Bake uncovered for 1 hour and 15 minutes until chicken is tender.

Serve with a tossed green salad and warm bread.

• OVEN FRIED CHICKEN •
(SHAKED AND BAKED)

I know. You can get this in a box at the supermarket. But why? Create your own from readily available ingredients in your spice cabinet. Tweak it as you like. Want a little more heat? Add a pinch or two of cayenne pepper. A touch of Italy? Replace the thyme with oregano and/or basil. Or add a 1/2 teaspoon of chili powder or cumin for a south-of-the-border nuance if that piques your fancy. Experiment and enjoy!

PREP: 10 minutes   COOK: 40 minutes

INGREDIENTS
- 1/4 cup flour
- 1/2 cup dried breadcrumbs
- 1/2 teaspoon Hungarian paprika
- 1/2 teaspoon onion powder
- 1/4 teaspoon garlic powder
- 1/4 teaspoon dried thyme
- 1/4 teaspoon kosher salt
- 1/8 teaspoon freshly ground pepper
- 6 chicken drumsticks (also good with thighs)
- 1/3 cup milk or buttermilk

DIRECTIONS
1. Preheat oven to 400°.

2. Combine flour, breadcrumbs, paprika, salt, onion powder, garlic powder, thyme, salt and pepper in plastic bag.

3. Dip chicken in milk and shake off excess. Add to bag and shake to coat evenly.

4. Coat a small baking sheet with cooking spray and add chicken. Bake 20 minutes, turn chicken pieces and bake another 20 minutes until chicken is tender and coating crisp.

Serve with Garlic Smashed Potatoes and Green Beans Amandine.

• CHICKEN AND BROCCOLI STIR-FRY •

As in all stir-fry recipes, this one will cook quickly. Therefore, you must have all of your ingredients chopped, sliced, and near the stove. As I remember hearing one of my cooking instructors say, the key to stir-frying vegetables is not to cook them, but to threaten them. If you don't own a wok, don't feel the need to run out and purchase one right away. A good skillet will do just fine in the Table for Two kitchen.

PREP: 10 minutes   COOK: 15 minutes

INGREDIENTS
    2 boneless, skinless chicken breasts cut up into 1-inch cubes
    2 teaspoons canola or peanut oil
    2 cups fresh broccoli florets
    1/2 pound mushrooms, sliced
    4 scallions cut into 1-inch long pieces
    3 tablespoons soy sauce
    3 tablespoons rice wine or dry sherry
    1/2 teaspoon dry ginger
    1 teaspoon corn starch dissolved in 2 tablespoons water
    1 teaspoon sesame oil

DIRECTIONS
    1. Heat oil in a 10-inch skillet or wok over medium-high heat. Add chicken cubes and stir-fry until opaque, about 3 minutes. Remove to a bowl and set aside.

    2. Add broccoli florets and stir-fry for 2 minutes. Add mushrooms, scallions, soy sauce, rice wine/sherry and ginger. Stir-fry for 2-3 minutes. Add cornstarch mixture, stir, and then add reserved chicken. Cook, stirring until heated through and sauce has thickened. Sprinkle with sesame oil and serve.

Serve over Steamed White Rice.

• STIR-FRIED CHICKEN WITH TOASTED SESAME SEEDS •

Some chefs create a similar dish using untoasted sesame seeds. However, I believe toasting them creates a wonderful aroma that infuses the dish, so it's worth taking the few minutes to do so.

PREP: 5 minutes   COOK: 10 minutes

INGREDIENTS
    3 tablespoons sesame seeds
    2 tablespoons hot water
    3 tablespoons dry mustard
    1/2 cup soy sauce
    1 clove garlic, minced
    2 tablespoons canola or peanut oil
    2 – 3 boneless, skinless chicken breasts cut into 1-inch cubes
    1 tablespoon lemon juice
    Pepper to taste

INGREDIENTS

1. Place sesame seeds in a small skillet over medium-high heat and cook briefly until nicely brown and fragrant. Place seeds in a small bowl.

2. Dipping Sauce: Whisk the water, dry mustard, soy sauce, 2 tablespoons sesame seeds and garlic a small bowl and reserve.

3. Heat oil in a 10-inch skillet or wok over medium-high heat. Add chicken cubes and stir-fry 5 – 8 minutes until lightly brown and opaque. Sprinkle with pepper, lemon juice and remaining sesame seeds. Cook for 2 – 3 more minutes until heated through. Serve with mustard sauce as a dipping sauce.

Serve with Steamed White Rice and Glazed Carrots.

Beef

Beef

I know, I know - beef has gotten a bad rap over the past two decades, and pork even more so. It's true that Americans generally eat too much of everything, and beef is certainly part of that 'everything'. It seems that everyday we're bombarded with messages telling us that we eat too much meat and how this habit is having an incredibly negative effect on our hearts. If we're honest, we would admit that this is true. We do eat too much meat. And even though we *say* we are trying to eat healthier, the statistics prove the opposite. When fast food and casual restaurants added healthier alternatives to their menus, we voted with our wallets and stayed away from the 'heart healthy' options. Not long ago, I was in a casual restaurant owned by a national chain and had a yen for something vegetarian. I ordered one of my favorite items, their delicious, grilled veggie burger. Alas, it was no longer on the menu and I couldn't even order one 'on the sly'. So even though we say we want to eat healthier, our actions speak louder than words and our waistlines continue to grow.

On the positive side, beef is tasty, filling, and an excellent source of protein, vitamins and minerals. Beef is simple to prepare and can be very economical when it's on sale. The beef industry has even responded to our requests for healthier fare by breeding leaner cattle. There is no reason why beef cannot be part of a healthy diet; we just need to change some of our thinking about it. Gone are the days when meat was served 4 or 5 nights a week. And likewise, gone are the days when we figured on 3/4 of a pound or more per person. I grew up in a household where meat and potatoes were staples. We had a variety of chops, roasts, and stews throughout the week and on the weekends we had thick, juicy steaks. That was the norm. Today we know that regimen is not only unhealthy, it's uneconomical. I certainly can't afford it and my body will not endure it.

But I haven't given up on beef. I'm just pickier about my selections. I look for well-marbled USDA Choice; USDA Prime cuts are generally reserved for the high-end restaurant industry. I buy smaller portions of good steak rather than larger portions of mediocre steak. There's even a new kid on the block – the flat iron steak (more on that later). I also make good use of rubs and sauces. It's heavenly on my taste buds and it's easier on my heart - and my wallet. So here's to beef. Good beef. Buy it. Prepare it right. And enjoy.

GRILLED STEAK – THE BASICS

Nothing whets my appetite like the sight, sound, and aroma of a good steak sizzling on the grill. But emptying my wallet to dine on a fine porterhouse at the local upscale steak joint isn't always an option and I know it's the same for you. Not to worry. You can create a wonderful steak dinner in your own home at a fraction of the price.

Do you have a small grill or hibachi? Great. We're ready to go. If you don't have an outdoor grill, I've included an indoor grilling method that will rival most steakhouses in your community.

First, purchase the right steaks from your butcher or grocer: bright red, well-marbled, and at least 1" thick. T-bone, porterhouse, New York strip, rib eye, and filet mignon are all good cuts. For those times when you have a craving for a delicious but economical steak, look for a nice top sirloin or flat iron - they're usually half the price of the more expensive cuts. In fact, many beef connoisseurs rate flat irons above New York strips in both flavor and tenderness.

Here are two methods that will create a mouth-watering steak. Bookmark this page because many of the following steak recipes will refer back to these cooking methods.

OUTDOORS: CHAR-GRILLED STEAK

1. Remove the steaks from the refrigerator a 1/2 hour to an hour before cooking and pat dry with paper towels. Sprinkle with kosher salt and cracked pepper if you're not using a marinade.

2. Build a medium-hot charcoal fire and allow the coals to grey. When you can't hold your hand 3 inches above the grill for more than 2 or 3 seconds you know the fire is ready.

3. Grill the steaks without turning for 3 - 4 minutes, then turn and grill for an additional 3 - 4 minutes for medium rare. Add an additional minute or two for medium.

INDOORS: PAN-SEARED AND ROASTED STEAK

Many home cooks turn to their oven broiler to cook steaks indoors. While this appears to make sense - after all, a broiler simply and upside down grill -

the truth of the matter is that most home broilers don't get hot enough to do the job. Many home cooks pan-sear their steaks in a hot cast iron skillet to yield good results; in fact, this method is actually closer to grilling than oven-broiling is. Simply preheat the skillet over medium-high heat until the bottom begins to turn grey. This will take about 5 minutes. Sprinkle kosher salt into the skillet and add the steaks. Pan-sear for 3 minutes then turn to sear for an additional 3 minutes for medium-rare. But be warned, if you don't have a high-powered exhaust fan over your stove, you may find yourself running throughout the house waving a towel in front of the screaming smoke detectors. That doesn't make for a very romantic evening. Trust me on that one. I've been there. However, there is a better way to grill steaks indoors. Here's how:

INDOORS: SEARED AND ROASTED STEAK

1. Remove the steaks from the refrigerator a 1/2 hour to an hour before cooking and pat dry with paper towels. Sprinkle with kosher salt and cracked pepper if not using a marinade.

2. Preheat your oven to its highest setting (at least 500°) and place an oven rack in its lowest position (I'm able to rest mine on the oven floor).

3. Preheat a cast iron skillet over medium-high heat on your stove for 4 or 5 minutes until the bottom begins to turn grey and the pan begins to smoke. Don't use an aluminum or non-stick skillet for this. You'll ruin the pan.

4. Add the steaks and immediately transfer the skillet to the oven. Roast the steaks for 3 minutes then turn and continue cooking an additional 2 or 3 minutes for medium rare.

• STEAK WITH RED WINE SAUCE •

This sauce compliments all grilling steaks but it's particularly good with filet mignon. While a filet may be melt-in-your-mouth tender, it doesn't have much flavor on its own, which is why it's often wrapped in bacon. Preparing a red wine sauce, or any of the sauces that follow, is a nice, fairly low-fat alternative to bacon.

PREP: 5 minutes   COOK: 15 minutes

INGREDIENTS
    2 grilling steaks, 1" thick
    Salt and pepper to taste
    1 tablespoon unsalted butter, divided
    1-1/2 teaspoons minced shallots
    1/4 cup dry red wine
    1/4 cup beef broth
    2 tablespoons cornstarch
    2 tablespoons soy sauce

DIRECTIONS

1.   Season steaks with kosher salt and cracked pepper to taste.

2.   Grill or sear-and-roast steaks as above. Remove steaks to a plate and cover with another plate to keep warm.

3.   Melt 1/2 tablespoon of butter in the skillet over medium-high heat.* Add the shallots and sauté until wilted, about 2 – 3 minutes. Add the red wine and beef broth; bring to a boil.

4.   Dissolve the cornstarch in the soy sauce and stir into the broth. Cook for 2 or 3 minutes until slightly thickened. Swirl in the remaining butter. Spoon sauce over steaks.

* If you're pan-searing/roasting your steaks rare to medium-rare, you can prepare the sauce in the cast iron skillet. If you're roasting your steaks to medium-well to well-done, the brown bits remaining in the skillet may be too charred to create a clean tasting sauce. Prepare the sauce in a separate small skillet.

Serve with Garlic Smashed Potatoes and Herb Baked Tomatoes.

• STEAK WITH MUSTARD-CREAM SAUCE •

A slightly tart and delicious cream sauce, this also goes well with grilled lamb or pork chops.

PREP: 5 minutes   COOK: 15 minutes

INGREDIENTS
   2 grilling steaks, 1" thick
   Salt and pepper to taste
   2 tablespoons unsalted butter
   1 tablespoon chopped shallots or onions
   2 tablespoons cognac
   3/4 cup cream
   1-1/2 teaspoons Dijon mustard
   1-1/2 teaspoons chopped fresh parsley

DIRECTIONS

   1.   Season steaks with salt and pepper to taste

   2.   Grill or sear-and-roast steaks as above. Remove steaks to a plate and cover with another plate to keep warm.

   3.   Melt butter in the skillet over medium-high heat.* Add the shallots and sauté until wilted, about 2 – 3 minutes.

   4.   Add the cognac and heat; ignite fumes with a match. When flames die out, add the cream and bring to a boil. Cook and stir over high heat for 3 – 5 minutes.

   5.   Remove from heat and stir in mustard and any juices that may have accumulated around the steaks. Strain sauce over steaks, sprinkle with parsley, and serve.

* If you're pan-searing/roasting your steaks rare to medium-rare, you can prepare the sauce in the cast iron skillet. If you're roasting your steaks to medium-well to well-done, the brown bits remaining in the skillet may be too charred to create a clean tasting sauce. Prepare the sauce in a separate small skillet.

Serve with Baked Potatoes and Cauliflower with Parsley and Garlic.

• STEAK WITH MADEIRA WINE SAUCE •

A pleasant departure from the typical red wine sauce, the slightly sweet and savory taste of its fortified wine adds a nice touch to this, and other red meat recipes. Remember, you don't have to spend a lot on wines for cooking. There are many reasonably price California sherries, ports and Madeira wines and that will do just fine.

PREP: 5 minutes   COOK: 15 minutes

INGREDIENTS

2 grilling steaks, 1" thick	1/3 cup beef broth
Salt and pepper to taste	2 teaspoons unsalted butter, divided
1 tablespoon olive oil	
1 tablespoon minced shallots	1/2 teaspoon flour
1/4 cup Madeira wine	1 teaspoon chopped fresh parsley

DIRECTIONS

1. Season steaks with salt and pepper to taste.

2. Grill or sear-and-roast steaks as above. Remove steaks to a plate and cover with another plate to keep warm.

3. Add the olive oil and shallots.* Sauté until wilted, about 2 – 3 minutes. Add the Madeira and cook for about 1 - 2 minutes to slightly reduce.

4. Add the broth and bring to a boil. Cook, stirring, until reduced by about half.

5. Meanwhile, blend 1 teaspoon of butter with the flour in a small bowl then stir into the wine/broth mixture. Cook and whisk until sauce thickens.

6. Stir in remaining butter then strain over the steaks. Sprinkle with parsley and serve.

* If you're pan-searing/roasting your steaks rare to medium-rare, you can prepare the sauce in the cast iron skillet. If you're roasting your steaks to medium-well to well-done, the brown bits remaining in the skillet may be too charred to create a clean tasting sauce. Prepare the sauce in a separate small skillet.

Serve with Baked Potatoes and Green Beans with Walnuts.

• STEAK WITH RED PEPPER AND PARMESAN CHEESE •

This is a hearty bistro-style recipe. Be sure to use freshly grated cheese if possible, but grated and bagged Parmesan is permissible. Please avoid using canned, powdered Parmesan, unless of course you have an unusual craving for talcum powder.

PREP: 5 minutes   COOK: 15 minutes

INGREDIENTS
    2 grilling steaks, 1" thick
    Salt and pepper to taste
    2 tablespoons unsalted butter
    1/4 cup dry white wine
    2 tablespoons finely grated Parmesan cheese
    1/4 teaspoon red pepper flakes (or more to taste)
    1-1/2 tablespoons chopped fresh parsley

DIRECTIONS

1. Season steaks with salt and pepper to taste.

2. Grill or sear-and-roast steaks as above. Remove steaks to a plate and cover with another plate to keep warm.

3. Melt butter in the skillet over medium-high heat.* Add white wine and any juice that has accumulated around the steaks. Cook until all the liquid has nearly evaporated.

4. Place the steaks in the skillet and top each steak with the Parmesan cheese, red pepper and chopped parsley. Turn off heat and sprinkle steaks with any juice that remains in the skillet until cheese has slightly melted then serve.

*If you're pan-searing/roasting your steaks rare to medium-rare, you can prepare the sauce in the cast iron skillet. If you're roasting your steaks to medium-well to well-done, the brown bits remaining in the skillet may be too charred to create a clean tasting sauce. Prepare the sauce in a separate small skillet.

Serve with Rice with Wine and Tomatoes.

• STEAK DIANE •

Why 'Diane'? Some foodies propose that 19th century sauces made 'á la Diane' were dedicated to Diana, goddess of wild animals and hunting. This makes sense. Sauce Diane is first mentioned in the writings of Georges Auguste Escoffier at the turn of the century, but the Drake Hotel in New York City appears to be the most agreed upon source of Steak Diane's development. Some food historians thumb their noses at this and point to the Copacabana Palace Hotel in Rio de Janeiro. Regardless of its birthplace, this classic dish has always won raves due to the dramatic flambé presentation.

PREP: 5 minutes   COOK: 10 minutes

INGREDIENTS

2 filet mignon steaks
Salt and pepper to taste
1 tablespoon canola or peanut oil
2 tablespoons unsalted butter, divided
1-1/2 teaspoons chopped fresh chives
1 tablespoon cognac or brandy

1-1/2 tablespoons chopped
   fresh parsley
1/2 teaspoon Dijon mustard
1/4 teaspoon Worcestershire
   sauce
1 teaspoon beef broth

DIRECTIONS

1. Place filet mignon or sirloin steaks between two pieces of plastic or wax paper and carefully pound to about 1/4" thickness.

2. Season steaks with salt and pepper to taste.

3. Heat the oil and 1 tablespoon butter in a small cast iron skillet over high heat. Add steaks and cook about 1-1/2 to 2 minutes on the first side and 30 seconds on the second side. Transfer steaks to a plate and cover with another plate to keep warm.

4. Add chives and cook for 10 seconds then stir in the cognac. Tilt the pan slightly and let the flame catch the cognac's vapors to ignite. (If your stove is electric, light the fumes with a match). Add the parsley, mustard, Worcestershire sauce and beef broth. Swirl in remaining tablespoon of butter. Pour sauce over steaks and serve.

Serve with Baked Potatoes and Steamed Squash with Sun Dried Tomatoes.

Flat Iron Steak –
And now for something completely different (almost).

Mention the name 'Flat Iron Steaks' to butchers a generation ago and they would probably lump it together with 'Lollipop Steaks', 'Saturday Night Steaks', 'Sizzler Steaks', and other creative names for less-than-tender cuts of meat that they needed to move out from behind the meat counter.

But those butchers of yesteryear would be wrong. While names like 'Lollipop Steaks' were simply creative nomenclatures given to cheap cuts of beef to command a higher price, the flat iron steak is different - very different.

The beef industry was looking for an affordable, tender, and flavorful alternative to the traditional, but increasingly expensive, grilling cuts. The result? The flat iron – a steak 'created' by researchers at the University of Florida and the University of Nebraska. Cut from the shoulder of the steer and originally known as 'top blade', this cut has a large band of connective tissue running through its center, thus rendering it a tough steak. But the researchers created a technique that removes the tendon and transforms this lowly cut of beef into one that's finding its way onto many top steakhouse menus. Many gourmands praise the flat iron for a tenderness that rivals filet mignon, yet retains the full-flavored, beefy character of a sirloin steak.

Why 'flat iron'? Because it looks like an old-fashioned metal iron, uniform in thickness and rectangular in shape. The flat iron's shape and size is an almost perfect cut for the Table for Two.

• HERB MARINATED FLAT IRON STEAK •

This, and all of the flat iron recipes work equally as well with flank steaks and skirt steaks. Adjust your cooking time based on the thickness. Flank steak will cook in about the same time as the flat iron, but the thinner skirt steak will be ready much sooner so plan on 2 minutes per side for medium-rare.

PREP: 5 minutes   MARINATE: 2 to 24 hours
COOK: 6 to 8 minutes

INGREDIENTS

12 ounce flat iron steak
1 tablespoon olive oil
1 clove garlic, minced
1/2 teaspoon chopped fresh parsley
1/2 teaspoon chopped rosemary
1/4 teaspoon chopped fresh chives
2 tablespoons dry red wine
1/4 teaspoon kosher salt
1/4 teaspoon black pepper
1/2 teaspoon dry mustard

DIRECTIONS

1. Combine the olive oil, garlic, parsley, rosemary, chives, red wine, salt, pepper, and mustard powder in a small bowl.

2. Place the steak in a re-sealable plastic bag and pour in marinade. Marinate in the refrigerator for at least 2 hours, turning each 1/2 hour, or overnight.

3. Remove steaks and pat dry.

4. Grill or sear-and-roast steaks as above about 3 minutes per side for medium-rare. Remove steaks to a plate and cover with another plate and allow to rest for about 5 minutes before serving.

Serve with Rice Pilaf with Pine Nuts and Raisins along with Steamed Asparagus.

• CAJUN FLAT IRON STEAK •

This one will waken your taste buds. Cut back on the hot sauce, lime juice and Cajun blackening seasoning if this is too much for you. Of course then you'll have to change the name from Cajun Flat Iron Steak to something along the lines of Humdrum Flat Iron Steak.

PREP: 10 minutes   MARINATE: 2 hours
COOK: 6 to 8 minutes

INGREDIENTS
    12 ounce flat iron steak
    2 teaspoons hot pepper sauce
    1 tablespoon lime juice
    1 clove garlic, minced
    1-1/2 teaspoons Cajun blackening seasoning
    1 teaspoon kosher salt
    1/8 teaspoon black pepper
    4 tablespoons unsalted butter
    1/3 cup beef broth

DIRECTIONS
1. Combine the hot pepper sauce, lime juice, garlic, Cajun seasoning, salt and pepper in a small bowl.

2. Place the steak in a re-sealable plastic bag and pour in marinade. Marinate in the refrigerator for at least 2 hours, turning each 1/2 hour, or overnight. Remove steak and pat dry.

3. Grill or sear-and-roast steaks as above about 3 minutes per side for medium rare. Remove steaks to a plate, cover with another plate and allow to rest for about 5 minutes before serving.

4. Stir butter and broth into a small saucepan over medium-high heat. Bring to a boil and reduce by about half. Season with additional salt and pepper to taste. Drizzle sauce over steaks and serve.

Serve with Orange Rice and Sautéed Glazed Tomatoes.

• FLAT IRON STEAK WITH HONEY •
AND BALSAMIC VINEGAR

I love the interplay between the concentrated sweetness of the honey and the complex flavor of a good balsamic vinegar.

PREP: 5 minutes   MARINATE: 2+ hours or over night
COOK: 6 – 8 minutes

INGREDIENTS
- 12 ounce flat iron steak
- 2 tablespoons honey
- 2 tablespoons balsamic vinegar
- 2 tablespoons red wine
- 2 tablespoons olive oil
- 1 tablespoon lemon juice
- 1/4 teaspoon tarragon
- 1/2 teaspoon kosher salt
- 1/4 teaspoon fresh ground pepper

DIRECTIONS
1. Combine honey, vinegar, wine, olive oil, lemon juice, tarragon, salt and pepper in a small bowl.

2. Put steak in a re-sealable plastic bag and pour marinade over steak. Marinate in the refrigerator for at least 2 hours, turning each 1/2 hour, or overnight.

3. Grill or sear-and-roast steaks as above about 3 minutes per side for medium rare. Remove steaks to a plate, cover with another plate and allow to rest for about 5 minutes before serving.

Serve with Mashed Potatoes and Creamed Carrots.

• LONDON BROIL •

Don't be misled. London broil is a method for cooking beef and not a particular cut. I know, I know, your neighborhood supermarket has cuts of beef in the case that are labeled London Broil (as does mine). But it's just a marketing ploy to sell less tender cuts of meat like the round. Opt for a good flank steak over those labeled London Broil and you'll never be disappointed.

PREP: 5 minutes   COOK: 15 minutes

INGREDIENTS
    12 ounce flank steak
    1 clove garlic, halved and peeled
    1 tablespoon olive oil
    Salt and pepper to taste
    1-1/2 tablespoons unsalted butter
    1 tablespoon chopped fresh parsley

DIRECTIONS
1. Rub the flank steak with the garlic and then rub with the olive oil. Season with salt and a generous amount of pepper.

2. Grill or sear-and-roast steaks as above about 3 - 4 minutes per side for medium rare.

3. Remove steak to a warm plate, dot with butter and sprinkle with parsley. Let stand 5 minutes. Slice across the diagonal and serve with juices that have accumulated around the steak.

Serve with Rice Pilaf and Glazed Carrots.

• BASIC POT ROAST •

As with any roast recipe, this classic will provide you with delicious leftovers for lunch. Just be sure to reheat the meat in a little broth or stock to keep it tender and moist.

PREP: 10 minutes   COOK: 1-1/2 to 2-1/2 hours

INGREDIENTS
2 – 3 pounds chuck or rump roast
1 clove garlic, slivered
1 bay leaf, finely crumbled
Salt and pepper to taste
4 large red potatoes
1 cup baby carrots
1 yellow onion
2 celery stalks
1/4 cup red wine or water
1/2 cup beef broth

DIRECTIONS

1. Poke several holes in the roast with a thin knife and insert the garlic slivers. Mix the crumbled the bay leaf with salt and pepper and rub all over the roast. Cut the potatoes, onion and celery into large chunks.

2. Heat the olive oil in a medium Dutch oven over medium-high heat. And the roast and brown on all sides. Remove the meat and add the vegetables. Sauté until they are softened and lightly browned, about 10 minutes.

3. Add the wine and deglaze, scraping the bottom of the pan, until the wine is nearly evaporated. Add broth. Return the roast to the pot and turn the heat to low. Cover and simmer, turning the roast every 15 to 20 minutes, until the roast can be easily pierced with a fork, about 1-1/2 to 2-1/2 hours.

4. Remove the roast and turn the heat to high. Cook until the remaining liquid thickens. Slice the roast thin and serve with the vegetables and pan juices.

• BRAISED SHORT RIBS •

Short ribs are usually the ends cut from the prime rib. They are very flavorful but must be cooked in liquid for an extended period of time to render them tender.

PREP: 10 minutes   COOK: 2-1/2 hours

INGREDIENTS
  1-1/2 pounds short ribs
  1/4 teaspoon thyme, marjoram or sage
  Salt and pepper to taste
  1 tablespoon olive oil
  1/3 cup beef broth
  1/3 cup stewed tomatoes
  2 tablespoons dry red wine
  1 clove garlic, minced
  3 red potatoes, peeled and cubed
  2 onions, chopped
  3 carrots, chopped
  2 teaspoons all-purpose flour
  1-1/2 tablespoon water

DIRECTIONS
  1. Heat the oil in a medium Dutch oven over medium-high heat. Add the ribs and season with salt, pepper and herb of choice. Brown well on all sides, taking care that they do not burn. This could take 15 to 20 minutes.

  2. Add the beef broth, tomatoes and garlic and bring to a boil. Reduce heat to low, cover, and simmer for 1-1/2 hours, adding more broth if necessary.

  3. Place the potatoes, onions, and carrots in the pot. Continue to simmer for another 30 minutes to 1 hour, or until all vegetables are tender. Remove the meat and vegetables to a serving platter.

  4. In a separate small bowl, dissolve the flour in the water. Add this to the pot and stir well until thickened. Pour over meat and vegetables.

• BRAISED SHORT RIBS WITH POTATOES AND MUSTARD •

PREP: 10 minutes   COOK: 2 hours

INGREDIENTS
- 1-1/2 pounds short ribs
- 1 tablespoon olive oil
- Salt and pepper to taste
- 3/4 cup minced onions
- 1 clove garlic, minced
- 1 cup beef broth
- 1/2 pound small red potatoes (halved, if large)
- 1 tablespoon Dijon mustard
- Fresh chopped parsley to garnish

DIRECTIONS

1. Heat the oil in a medium Dutch oven over medium-high and brown the ribs well on all sides, seasoning them with salt and pepper. Take care that they do not burn. This could take 15 to 20 minutes.

2. Remove the ribs and keep warm. Pour off all but 1 tablespoon of the fat and lower the heat to medium. Add the onions and sauté until soft and translucent, about 8 minutes. Add the garlic and sauté 1 additional minute.

3. Pour in the broth and return the ribs to the pot and raise heat to medium-high. Bring to a boil, cover and return heat to low. Cook stirring occasionally for 30 minutes.

4. Add the potatoes and cook, stirring occasionally every 15 minutes, adding additional broth if the mixture gets too dry. Cook until the ribs are falling-off-the-bone tender, at least 30 – 45 minutes or more. Stir in the mustard and garnish with chopped parsley.

Serve with Green Beans Niçoise.

• BEEF BURGUNDY •

If you make this a day ahead of time the flavors will meld and you'll have a truly heavenly dish. Can't make it ahead of time? Don't worry. This recipe is for four. That way, you'll have enough left over for lunch tomorrow.

PREP: 10 minutes   MARINATE: 8 to 24 Hours
COOK: 2 to 2-1/2 hours

INGREDIENTS
   2 pounds boneless chuck or bottom round cut into 1-1/2 inch chunks

For the marinade:
   1 cup burgundy wine
   2 tablespoons olive oil
   1 small onion chopped
   1 small carrot chopped
   1 clove garlic chopped
   1 bay leaf
   1 tablespoon chopped fresh parsley
   1/4 teaspoon thyme
   1/2 teaspoon cracked pepper
   1/4 teaspoon kosher salt

To finish:
   1 slice of bacon, diced
   1 tablespoon olive oil
   1 tablespoon flour
   1 cup beef broth
   1/2 (15.5-ounce) can diced tomatoes
   4 ounces mushrooms, quartered
   1/2 cup pearl onions, peeled
   2 tablespoons chopped fresh parsley

DIRECTIONS

1. Mix marinade ingredients in a bowl. Place meat in a 1-gallon plastic bag and add marinade. Toss to coat and place in the refrigerator for up to 24 hours. Turn occasionally.

2. Remove the beef and pat dry. Strain the marinade into a bowl and reserve the vegetables in another bowl.

3. Heat a Dutch oven over medium-high heat and add the bacon. Cook until brown and remove the bacon. Add the olive oil and heat. Add the beef and brown on all sides (you'll need to do this in batches so the meat will brown, rather than steam). Remove with a slotted spoon to a bowl.

4. Add the reserved vegetables, stir and cook until slightly brown, 5 minutes or so.

5. Add the flour and stir for 1 – 2 minutes until smooth and slightly brown. Stir in the reserved marinade, beef broth, and tomatoes. Return the beef and bacon to the pan. Bring to a boil and cover. Reduce the heat and simmer for 1-1/2 to 2 hours until meat is very tender but not falling apart.

6. Add mushrooms and onions and cover. Cook an additional 15 – 20 minutes until tender. Garnish with fresh parsley.

• CHILI CON CARNE •

The correct method for making chili con carne is hotly debated across the country. It seems that every county has its own Chili Cook-Off. Here is a very basic and simple recipe. Commit this to memory then experiment. Remember, there is no such thing as bad chili as long as it is hot and it is red.

PREP: 5 minutes   COOK: 2 to 3 hours

INGREDIENTS
    3 tablespoons olive oil
    1 large onion, minced
    2 garlic cloves, minced
    2 pounds lean ground beef
    1 (14.5-ounce) can diced tomatoes
    1 green pepper, minced
    1 cup beef broth
    2 tablespoons chili powder
    1 teaspoon ground cumin
    1/2 teaspoon kosher salt
    1/2 teaspoon celery seed
    1/8 teaspoon cayenne pepper (or more to taste)
    1 teaspoon oregano
    1/4 teaspoon basil
    1 bay leaf

DIRECTIONS
1. Heat oil in a Dutch oven over medium heat. Add onions and sauté until soft and lightly brown, about 10 minutes. Add garlic and sauté for 1 minute. Add the ground beef and stir until brown.

2. Add the remaining ingredients, bring to a boil, reduce heat and simmer, uncovered until the sauce is as thick as you desire, 2 to 3 hours.

• CINCINNATI CHILI •

Cincinnati Chili, with its hint of chocolate (yes, chocolate!), is unusual *and* delicious. While most versions of chili are ladled into large bowls, Cincinnati Chili is traditionally served over cooked spaghetti then topped with chopped onions, grated cheddar cheese, and oyster crackers.

PREP: 10 minutes   COOK: 3 hours

INGREDIENTS

2 pounds lean ground beef
1 tablespoon olive oil
2 medium onions, chopped
4 garlic cloves, minced
4 cups beef broth
1 (15.5-ounce) can tomato sauce
1 tablespoon cider or white wine vinegar
1 tablespoon Worcestershire sauce
1 teaspoon ground allspice

1/4 teaspoon ground cloves
1/2 teaspoon ground cumin
1/2 teaspoon cayenne pepper
   or to taste
3 tablespoons chili powder
1 bay leaf
1/2 ounce unsweetened
   chocolate, grated

DIRECTIONS

1. Heat the olive oil in a Dutch oven over medium heat. Add the ground beef and cook until no longer pink. Remove with a slotted spoon to a bowl. Pour off all but 1 tablespoon fat.

2. Add the onions and sauté until soft and lightly brown, about 8 -10 minutes. Add the garlic and sauté for 1 minute.

3. Return the meat to the pot and add the broth, tomato sauce, vinegar and Worcestershire sauce. Return to a boil, reduce heat and simmer for 1/2 hour.

4. Add the allspice, cloves, cumin, cayenne pepper, chili powder, bay leaf and chocolate. Return to a boil, cover and reduce heat to low. Simmer for at least 1 hour. (Some cooks let it simmer for as much as 2-1/2 to 3 hours). Check occasionally and add more broth if necessary.

Serve over cooked spaghetti.

• PICADILLO •

This traditional Cuban recipe is said to be the forerunner of the American Sloppy Joe. Rumor has it this stewed ground meat dish was first served between two slices of bread at Sloppy Joe's Bar in Key West. The rest, as they say, is history. Is the claim true? Who knows? But whether served on a bun or over white rice with a side of black beans, this Latin American classic is a deliciously different Sloppy Joe for the Table for Two.

PREP: 10 minutes   COOK: 30 minutes

INGREDIENTS

1 pound ground beef
1 teaspoon ground cumin
1 teaspoon kosher salt
1 teaspoon freshly ground pepper
1 tablespoon olive oil
1 onion, chopped
1/2 green pepper, chopped
3 garlic cloves, minced
1 (14.5-ounce) can chopped tomatoes with juice

10 pimento-stuffed green
   olives, finely chopped
2 tablespoons raisins
2 tablespoons capers, drained
1 hard boiled egg white,
   chopped (optional)
4 bananas, sliced, to garnish

DIRECTIONS

1. Combine the ground beef, cumin, salt and pepper in a bowl and let sit for 5 minutes.

2. Heat the olive oil in a 10-inch skillet over medium-high heat. Sauté the onions, peppers and garlic until the onions are soft and lightly brown, about 8 minutes.

3. Add the beef, stir and cook until brown. Add the tomatoes, olives, raisins, and capers. Cook, stirring until nearly all of the liquid has evaporated. About 6 to 8 minutes. The mixture should be moist.

4. Add the egg white and stir to heat. Spoon the mixture onto a serving platter with the rice. Garnish with the sliced bananas.

Serve over Steamed White Rice.

• THE PERFECT HAMBURGER •

You've probably seen articles titled *The Secret to Grilling the Perfect Hamburger* or something close to that. How can there be any secrets to such a simple and widespread dish? Who's keeping those secrets anyway? If cooking a great hamburger is a secret, why are they blabbing about it in national magazines? Truth is that there are no secrets. The recipe for the perfect hamburger includes good ingredients and a touch of common sense.

First, start with the right cut of beef. Chuck is preferred due to its fat-to-lean ratio. If you have the capacity, coarsely grind it yourself in a food processor. If that is not an option, then purchase fresh-ground chuck from your market that grinds its meat daily. Try to avoid mass produced ground meat if possible due to recent reports of widespread contamination by salmonella and e-coli bacteria. Even though the risk of contamination is relatively small compared to the amount of ground beef American's consume, why take the risk if you have a viable option?

Like many of the preceding steak recipes, hamburgers do not have to be made on a grill. A pre-heated cast iron skillet, sprinkled with salt, will also produce a magnificent burger.

INGREDIENTS:
    3/4 pound ground chuck
    1/2 teaspoon (or more) salt
    Fresh ground pepper to taste

DIRECTIONS:
1. Loosely mix the meat with the salt and pepper in a small bowl. Divide the meat into two equal and loosely-packed balls (use a scale if necessary). You want the burgers to cook at an even rate. Press the meat into patties about 3/4 of an inch thick. Avoid handling the patties too much. Press a small indentation in the center of each patty with your thumb. (This will insure an evenly shaped final burger).

2. Preheat a coal or gas grill to medium, or pre-heat a cast iron skillet over medium-high heat for 2-3 minutes. Sprinkle the pan with kosher salt.

3. Add the burgers and cook for 5-7 minutes for medium-rare or 7-9 minutes for medium, flipping the burgers half way through. Do not press the patties down with a spatula as they cook.

4. If you are making cheeseburgers, add the cheese after you remove the burgers from the grill. The heat of the burgers will melt the cheese (and who wants to clean melted cheese from the grill or skillet anyway?).

Great ideas to enhance your burger experience:

- Bleu Cheese Burger: Add 3/4 ounce crumble blue with a 1/4-teaspoon Worcestershire sauce and 1/8 teaspoon dry mustard to the seasoned ground beef before forming patties.

- Philly Burger: Add 1-1/4 teaspoons Worcestershire sauce, 1 clove garlic, minced, 3 tablespoons minced onion, and 1/2 teaspoon Italian-style herbs to the seasoned ground beef.

- Tex-Mex Burger: Add 2 tablespoons minced onion, 1 tablespoon bottled salsa, 1/2 teaspoon chili powder (or more to taste), and 1/4 teaspoon dried oregano to seasoned ground beef.

Pork

 ## Pork

Folks have been eating pork for a long, long time. The pig is one of the oldest forms of domesticated livestock. Ancient cultures in the near East and China domesticated pigs as early as 7000 BC. And while they were mostly used for food, people also used the hides for shields and shoes, the bones for tools and weapons, and the bristles for brushes. Today, the medical community even uses pig flesh for human skin grafts and heart valves in transplants. So unless you are a vegan, you would be hardpressed to not call our little four-footed friend a blessing.

If you're like me, you may be surprised to learn that pork is the most widely eaten meat in the world. According to the USDA's Foreign Agricultural Service, nearly 100 million metric tons of pork were consumed worldwide in 2006.

Contrary to popular opinion, pigs are not filthy, nor do they sweat. Sure, you may see them rolling around in mud, but this helps them cool down and keeps them free of parasites. Pigs are also the only farm animals that designate a spot away from their living areas to relieve themselves. That's better than some humans I've met.

Today pork is marketed as 'the other white meat'. However, the USDA and most nutritional studies group pork with red meat such as beef. Is this simply a form of creative marketing? Perhaps. Can pork be part of a healthy diet? You bet. Most of the cuts of pork presented in the pages below are as lean as skinless chicken and are a good source of protein, thiamin, vitamin B6, phosphorus, niacin, riboflavin, potassium, and zinc.

Unfortunately, at least taste-wise, today's pork is much leaner than that of our forebears. The days of grilling well-marbled pork chops in the frying pan are over - unless your palate leans toward dry and tough. Fortunately, there are new ways to prepare pork that will render a succulent entrée that is not only mouthwatering, but good for you as well. Enjoy!

• GRILLED PORK TENDERLOIN WITH DIJON MUSTARD •

Pork tenderloin is a perfect cut for the Table for Two kitchen. Believe it or not, it's lower in fat than almost any other meat and it can be cooked in a jiffy. The downside? Like chicken breasts, the tenderloin does not have much flavor. However, it takes to marinating very well and if you place the tenderloin in the marinade before heading off to work or another activity, you'll have a remarkable dinner on the table in under half an hour.

PREP: 5 minutes   MARINATE: 4+ hours
COOK: 25 minutes

INGREDIENTS
  1/3 cup honey
  1/4 cup Dijon mustard
  1/4 teaspoon chili powder
  1/4 teaspoon kosher salt
  3/4 pound pork tenderloin

DIRECTIONS

1. Combine the honey, Dijon mustard, chili powder, and salt in a small bowl. Place meat in a re-sealable plastic bag. Pour marinade over tenderloin, seal, and refrigerate for at least 4 hours.

2. Prepare the grill for indirect heat.

3. Lightly oil grill grate. Remove meat from marinade and pat dry. Grill for 15 to 25 minutes to desired doneness (145°). Remove from grill, cover and let sit for 10 minutes before carving into 1/2 inch thick slices.

Alternative: Though not optimal, you can preheat oven to 350° and place pork on a rack in a shallow baking dish. Roast to for 45 minutes or until a meat thermometer reads 145°

Serve with Rice with Pine Nuts and Raisins along with Sesame Green Beans.

• SWEET BOURBON PORK TENDERLOIN •

Once you try this and other tenderloin recipes, you'll find yourself doubling them for a great luncheon meal the next day.

PREP: 5 minutes   MARINATE: 4+ hours
COOK: 45 minutes

INGREDIENTS
    2 tablespoons soy sauce
    2 tablespoons bourbon
    2 teaspoons brown sugar
    1 clove garlic, halved
    3/4 pound pork tenderloin

DIRECTIONS
1. Combine the soy sauce, bourbon, brown sugar, and garlic in a small bowl. Place meat in a re-sealable plastic bag. Pour marinade over tenderloin, seal, and refrigerate for at least 4 hours.

2. Preheat oven to 325°. Remove pork from marinade and place on rack in a shallow roasting pan.

3. Bake for 45 minutes or until meat thermometer registers 145°. Remove from oven and cover loosely. Allow to sit for 10 minutes before carving into 1/2-inch slices.

Note: This dish is also excellent grilled.

Serve with Dutch Potatoes and Broccoli with Garlic and Red Pepper.

• BISTRO PORK TENDERLOIN •

You must think that I eat nothing but pork tenderloin. That's nonsense. Well, almost.

PREP: 10 minutes   COOK: 40 minutes

INGREDIENTS
   1 tablespoon unsalted butter
   1 clove garlic, peeled and minced
   3/4 pound pork tenderloin, cut into 1/2" by 2" strips
   3/4 cup canned diced tomatoes with green chilies
   1/2 teaspoon dried basil
   1 teaspoon kosher salt
   1/2 teaspoon freshly ground black pepper
   1 tablespoon extra virgin olive oil
   1/2 green bell pepper, thinly sliced
   1/2 red bell pepper, thinly sliced
   1 medium onion, sliced

DIRECTIONS
1. Melt butter in a 10-inch skillet over medium-high heat. Add garlic and sauté for 1 minute. Arrange tenderloin strips in one layer. Cook, turning occasionally, until browned on both sides.

2. Stir in tomatoes and season with basil, salt, and pepper. Cook until mixture comes to a boil. Reduce heat to low, and cover.

3. Meanwhile, heat olive oil in another skillet over medium heat. Sauté peppers and onion until vegetables are tender-crisp, about 8 minutes.

4. Stir peppers and onions into pork tenderloin and tomatoes. Continue cooking until pork tenderloin strips are melt-in-your-mouth tender, about 20 - 30 minutes.

Serve with Roasted Red Potatoes and Grilled Tomatoes with Garlic and Rosemary.

• PORK TENDERLOIN WITH CREAMY HERB SAUCE •

I make this with light cream, but if your taste runs to a thicker and richer sauce, prepare this with butter instead of the olive oil and substitute regular or heavy cream.

PREP: 5 minutes   COOK: 30 minutes

INGREDIENTS
- 2 teaspoons olive oil
- 1/4 cup minced carrots
- 3/4 pound pork tenderloin, cut into medallions
- 1 teaspoon all-purpose flour
- 1-1/2 teaspoons dried basil
- 1 tablespoon chopped fresh parsley
- 1/4 teaspoon ground black pepper
- 1/3 cup light cream
- 2 tablespoons dry white wine

DIRECTIONS
1. Heat oil in a 10-inch skillet over medium heat. Sauté carrots for 5 minutes. Add pork, and cook until lightly browned. Remove pork, and keep warm.

2. Add the flour, basil, parsley and pepper. Whisk in light cream, stirring until thick. Add the wine and stir. Return pork to pan, reduce heat to low, and cover. Simmer for 20 minutes, stirring occasionally.

Serve with Garlic Smashed Potatoes and Green Beans Amandine.

• PORK TENDERLOIN WITH SUN-DRIED TOMATO SAUCE •

This dish is very rich. You must use fresh herbs; dried will simply not do in this instance. When you begin to eat, you'll imagine yourself watching the sunset while dining at a rustic trattoria overlooking the Mediterranean.

PREP: 10 minutes   COOK: 35 minutes

INGREDIENTS
  1 tablespoon olive oil
  2 tablespoons chopped prosciutto (smoked ham may be used)
  1 tablespoon chopped fresh sage
  1 tablespoon chopped fresh parsley
  1 tablespoon chopped oil-packed sun-dried tomatoes
  1 small onion, chopped
  1 clove garlic, peeled and minced
  3/4 pound pork tenderloin, cut into 1/2" by 2" strips
  1/4 cup chicken broth
  1/4 cup cream
  1/4 teaspoon kosher salt
  1/4 teaspoon ground black pepper

DIRECTIONS
  1. Heat the oil in a skillet over medium-high heat. Sauté the prosciutto, sage, parsley, sun-dried tomatoes, onion, and garlic for 5 minutes, until onion is nearly tender. Add the pork strips and sauté until brown, about 10 minutes.

  2. Stir the broth and cream into the skillet and season with salt and pepper. Bring to a boil. Reduce heat to low, and simmer 20 minutes, stirring occasionally, until pork is light pink and the sauce has thickened.

Serve with Buttered Noodles and Steamed Brussels Sprouts.

• HAM STEAKS WITH MADEIRA AND MUSTARD SAUCE •

Ham steaks are the Rodney Dangerfield's of the meat department. They "don't get no respect", probably because the last time we had them was in our high school cafeteria where they'd been cooked until they had the taste and texture of shoe leather. This recipe will change your opinion of ham steak, like it did mine.

PREP: 10 minutes   COOK: 10 minutes

INGREDIENTS
   3/4 pound ham steak, 3/4 to 1-inch thick
   2 tablespoons unsalted butter, divided
   1 tablespoon minced shallot
   1 apple (Macintosh, if available) cored, peeled and quartered
   2 tablespoons Madeira wine
   1/2 teaspoon tomato paste
   1/2 teaspoon Dijon mustard

DIRECTIONS
   1.   Trim excess fat from the ham steak.

   2.   Heat the tablespoon butter in a 10-inch skillet over medium heat. Add the shallots and sauté for 1 minute.

   3.   Add the steak and arrange apple quarters around steak. Spoon 1 tablespoon Madeira over the apples. Cover and cook for 5 minutes. Transfer steak to a warm platter and arrange the apples around the steak. Cover lightly.

   4.   Add the remaining wine, tomato paste and mustard to the skillet. Stir and bring to a simmer. Swirl in the remaining butter and pour sauce over the steak.

Serve with Buttered Noodles with Carrots.

• BROILED HAM STEAK WITH APRICOT GLAZE •

Ham steaks, like chicken breasts, cook in a matter of minutes. They can be a nice alternative to chicken when time is short but you still want an out-of-the-ordinary meal. Ham steaks can be purchased in individual packages, which makes them convenient when you're stocking up for the week. Buy two and toss one in the freezer. It won't take up much room and you'll always have something on hand for an emergency meal.

PREP: 5 minutes   COOK: 15 minutes

INGREDIENTS
    3/4 pound ham steak, 3/4 to 1-inch thick
    1/2 cup apricot preserves
    1/4 cup red wine vinegar
    1/8 teaspoon ground cinnamon
    1 tablespoon minced fresh chili peppers (your choice: mild or hot)

DIRECTIONS
    1. Preheat broiler to high, set rack to 4 inches from the heating elements.

    2. Combine the apricot preserves, red wine vinegar, cinnamon and chili peppers in a small saucepan,. Cook until the mixture is slightly thickened.

    3. Brush one side of the steak with the glaze and broil, glazed side up, for 5 minutes. Turn the steak and brush with glaze. Broil for 5 minutes more.

Serve with Boiled New Potatoes and Cauliflower Polonaise.

• FUSION GRILLED PORK CHOPS •

These delicious chops are marinated in a unique blend of diverse flavors: soy sauce, chili sauce, lemon juice and brown sugar. Toss in a crushed garlic clove (or two) for a mouthwatering and tangy chop. Just make sure you purchase thick, center-cut chops; thin ones will dry out by the time they are cooked.

PREP: 10 minutes   MARINATE: 8+ hours
COOK: 20 minutes

INGREDIENTS
    2 center-cut pork chops, 1-inch thick
    3 tablespoons soy sauce
    1 tablespoon fresh lemon juice
    3/4 teaspoon brown sugar
    3/4 teaspoon chili sauce
    1 clove garlic, peeled and crushed

DIRECTIONS
1. Combine the soy sauce, lemon juice, brown sugar, chili sauce, and garlic in a small bowl. Place the pork chops into a re-sealable bag. Pour marinade over chops and refrigerate for 8 hours or overnight. Turn the bag over about halfway through.

2. Preheat an outdoor grill for high heat.

3. Arrange pork chops on the lightly oiled grate, and cook 5 to 7 minutes on each side, until the internal temperature reaches 160°.

Serve with Rice Pilaf and Stir Fried Snow Peas.

• PORK CHOPS WITH BURGUNDY MUSHROOM SAUCE •

Here is a pork chop recipe inspired by the famous Beef Burgundy. Feel free to add 6 – 8 pearl onions to the skillet when you add the wine for a nice touch.

PREP: 5 minutes   COOK: 35 minutes

INGREDIENTS
    1 tablespoon unsalted butter
    1 clove garlic, crushed
    1 cup sliced fresh mushrooms
    1-1/2 tablespoons Dijon mustard
    2 center-cut pork chops, 1-inch thick
    1/4 cup red wine
    1/4 cup beef broth
    6 – 8 pearl onions (optional)
    1/8 teaspoon thyme

DIRECTIONS
1. Melt butter in a 10-inch skillet over medium heat. Add the garlic and sauté for 1 minute. Add the mushrooms and sauté until they begin to lose their moisture. Remove mushrooms and set aside.

2. Spread mustard on each side of the pork chops. Add the chops to the skillet and brown on each side.

3. Add wine, broth and onions (if using) to skillet. Cover and cook 15-20 minutes or until chops are tender. Remove chops to serving platter and cover loosely.

4. Boil remaining liquid for 5 minutes to reduce. Stir in mushrooms then spoon sauce over chops.

Serve with Garlic Smashed Potatoes and Creamed Spinach.

• PORK CHOPS WITH ROSEMARY AND WHITE WINE

These marinated pork chops are also great on the grill. If the weather's nice, fire up the hibachi and cook for 10 or 12 minutes, turning once.

PREP: 10 minutes   MARINATE: 4+ hours
COOK: 30 minutes

INGREDIENTS
    2 center-cut pork loin chops, 1-inch thick
    1/4 cup soy sauce
    2 tablespoons white wine
    1-1/2 tablespoons brown sugar
    1-1/2 teaspoons dried rosemary, crushed

DIRECTIONS
1.   Preheat oven to 350°.

2.   Combine the soy sauce, wine, brown sugar and rosemary in a small bowl. Place meat in a re-sealable plastic bag. Pour marinade over chops and refrigerate for at least 4 hours, turning occasionally.

3.   Drain and discard marinade. Place the chops in a lightly oiled baking dish. Bake uncovered for 30-35 minutes or until juices run clear.

Serve with Roasted New Potatoes with Parmesan and Orange Glazed Carrots.

• PORK CHOPS WITH RASPBERRY SAUCE •

Like chicken, pork is another meat that does very well with fruit. Here I use raspberry jam, but strawberry jam will do just as well.

PREP: 5 minutes   COOK: 15 minutes

INGREDIENTS
- 1/4 teaspoon dried thyme
- 1/4 teaspoon dried sage
- 1/4 teaspoon kosher salt
- 1/8 teaspoon freshly ground pepper
- 2 center-cut pork loin chops, 1-inch thick
- 2 teaspoons unsalted butter
- 2 teaspoons olive oil
- 2 tablespoons seedless raspberry jam
- 1 tablespoon orange juice
- 1 tablespoon white wine vinegar
- 2 sprigs fresh thyme for garnish (optional)

DIRECTIONS

1. Combine the thyme, sage, salt and pepper in a small bowl. Rub evenly over pork chops.

2. Melt butter and olive oil in a 10-inch skillet over medium heat. Add pork chops and cook for 4 - 5 minutes on each side, until juices run slightly pink. Remove chops from skillet and place on a warm plate, cover.

3. Combine raspberry jam, orange juice, and vinegar in a small bowl and add to the skillet. Bring to a boil, and cook for 2 to 3 minutes, or until sauce is reduced to desired consistency (sauce will thicken as it cools). Spoon sauce in a pool onto a serving plate, and top with pork chops. Garnish with sprigs of thyme.

Serve with Mashed Potatoes and Simple Braised Carrots.

• PORK CHOPS WITH FRESH TOMATO AND FETA •

The rich and tangy feta adds a zesty nuance to this dish. If fresh grape tomatoes are not available, feel free to use diced canned tomatoes in their place.

PREP: 5 minutes   COOK: 20 minutes

INGREDIENTS
   3 tablespoons olive oil, divided
   1/2 large onion, halved and thinly sliced
   2 center-cut pork loin chops, 1-inch thick
   Salt and pepper to taste
   1 cup red grape tomatoes, halved
   2 cloves garlic, peeled and minced
   1-1/2 teaspoons dried basil
   1-1/2 teaspoons balsamic vinegar
   2 ounces feta cheese, crumbled

DIRECTIONS
1. Heat 1 tablespoon oil in a 10-inch skillet over medium-high heat. Sauté the onion until soft and translucent, about 8 minutes. Remove onion and set aside.

2. Heat 1 tablespoon oil in the skillet. Season pork chops with salt and pepper, and place in the skillet. Cook 4 to 5 minutes on each side. Set aside and keep warm.

3. Heat remaining oil in the skillet. Return onions to skillet, and stir in tomatoes, garlic and basil. Sauté until tomatoes are tender, about 3 – 5 minutes. Stir in balsamic vinegar and season with salt and pepper to taste.

4. Spoon the onion and tomato mixture over the chops then sprinkle with feta cheese.

Serve with Boiled New Potatoes and Brussels Sprouts in Garlic Butter.

• BASQUE PORK CHOPS •

Pork chops smothered in peppers and onions in a tomato-wine sauce is a
a staple in this colorful region of northern Spain. If you can find a good Spanish
Rioja wine, by all means use it to create an authentic dish. If that wine is
unavailable, feel free to use any good dry white wine.

PREP: 5 minutes   COOK: 35 minutes

INGREDIENTS
    2 center-cut pork loin chops, 1-inch thick
    Salt and pepper to taste
    1 tablespoon flour
    2 tablespoons olive oil, divided
    1 clove garlic, minced
    1/2 cup chopped onion
    1/2 green pepper, thinly sliced
    1/2 red pepper, thinly sliced
    2 tablespoons dry white wine
    1/2 cup diced tomatoes (canned is fine)
    1/4 cup chicken or vegetable broth
    1 small bay leaf
    1/4 teaspoon thyme

DIRECTIONS
1. Sprinkle chops with salt and pepper then dredge in flour and shake off
    excess.

2. Heat 1 tablespoon olive oil in a 10-inch skillet over medium-high heat.
    Add the chops and cook until browned, about 2 – 3 minutes per side.
    Remove the chops to a warm plate and cover.

3. Wipe out the skillet and add remaining olive oil. Add the garlic, onions
    and peppers and sauté for 1 minute. Add the wine and sauté for 1
    minute. Add the tomatoes, broth, bay leaf and thyme. Bring to a boil and
    top with the pork chops. Reduce heat, cover and simmer for 25 minutes
    or until tender.

4. Remove the chops to a serving plate. Discard bay leaf and pour the
    sauce over the chops to serve.

Serve with Oven Fries and Steamed Squash with Sun-Dried Tomatoes.

• PORK LOIN ROAST FLORENTINE •

You'll notice that I recommend Garlic Smashed Potatoes and Sautéed Spinach with this recipe, but sometimes I'll simply toss in a few chunked red potatoes, carrots and onion for the last hour of cooking to make a terrific one-dish meal. I also like to double this recipe so I have some pork available for the next day. Slice it thin and place between slices of country bread to make wonderful sandwiches.

PREP: 10 minutes   COOK: 1-1/2 hours

INGREDIENTS
  1 clove garlic, minced
  1 teaspoon dried rosemary
  1/2 teaspoon fennel seeds, crushed or ground
  1/4 teaspoon kosher salt
  1/4 teaspoon freshly ground pepper
  3/4 pound boneless pork loin roast
  1 tablespoon olive oil
  2 tablespoons white wine

DIRECTIONS
  1. Preheat oven to 450°.

  2. Crush garlic with rosemary, salt and pepper to make a paste. Pierce meat with a sharp knife in several places and press the half the garlic paste into the incisions. Rub meat with the remaining garlic paste and olive oil and place in a shallow roasting pan.

  3. Roast at 450° for 10 minutes then reduce the oven temperature to 250°. Continue to cook until a meat thermometer inserted in the center registers 150° to 155° (about 45 to 80 minutes depending on the size of the roast). Remove pork loin to a cutting board and cover loosely.

  4. Add the wine to the pan and stir to loosen browned bits of food on the bottom. Serve with pan juices.

Serve with Garlic Smashed Potatoes and Sautéed Spinach.

• ROAST PORK LOIN WITH HERBED POTATOES •

I like this recipe because it is easy to double for company. The prep time is easy and once completed, the roast can be popped into the oven until company arrives. Even the Creamed Peas with Mushrooms can be prepared in advance and reheated at the last minute.

PREP: 20 minutes   COOK: 2 hours

INGREDIENTS
    3 medium all-purpose potatoes, peeled and quartered
    2 teaspoons olive oil
    1/2 teaspoon dried thyme, divided
    3 cloves garlic, crushed, divided
    1/2 teaspoon chopped fresh chives
    1 small onion, chopped
    Salt and pepper to taste
    3/4 pound boneless pork loin roast

DIRECTIONS
1.   Preheat oven to 350°.

2.   Place the potatoes in a pot with enough water to cover. Bring to a boil and cook until barely tender, about 10 minutes. Drain, cool, and place in a bowl. Toss with olive oil, 1/4 teaspoon thyme, 1 clove garlic, chives, and salt and pepper to taste.

3.   Combine the remaining thyme, garlic cloves and onion in a small bowl. Rub the pork loin roast with the mixture then sprinkle with salt and pepper.

4.   Place the roast on a rack in a shallow roasting pan and cook 50 minutes. Arrange the potatoes around the roast, and continue cooking 50 minutes to an internal temperature of 150° to 155°. Remove from oven, cover with foil, and let sit 15 minutes before slicing.

Serve with Creamed Peas with Mushrooms.

• ROAST PORK LOIN WITH HERBS, GARLIC AND BACON •

Once this roast hits the oven it will begin to release a wonderful aroma. If you were not hungry when you began to prepare it, I guarantee you will be ravenous by the time it is done. It smells that good.

PREP: 5 minutes   COOK: 2 hours

INGREDIENTS
    3/4 pound pork loin roast
    1 teaspoon olive oil
    2 slices bacon, cut in half
    2/3 cup chicken stock
    1/2 teaspoon rosemary
    1/2 teaspoon thyme
    1/2 teaspoon basil
    1/2 teaspoon rubbed sage
    1 clove garlic, chopped
    6 - 8 pearl onions, peeled (frozen is fine)

DIRECTIONS
1.   Preheat the oven to 300°.

2.   Rub the pork loin with olive oil and place in a small roasting pan. Drape slices of bacon over the top. Combine the chicken stock, rosemary, thyme, basil, sage and garlic in a small bowl and pour over the roast. Place onions around the sides. Cover with a lid or aluminum foil.

3.   Bake for 1 hour and 30 minutes. Remove the lid or foil, and continue to bake for 30 minutes, or until the bacon is browned.

Serve with Rice and Wine and Tomatoes.

• TANGY BABY BACK RIBS •

Baby back ribs are cut from the loin. They have more meat on them than standard spareribs, but they also have less fat and therefore less flavor. However, baby backs are just the right size for a Table for Two meal, particularly if you're watching your saturated fat intake. This tangy rub, with accompanying sauce, will more than make up for the missing fat. Feel free to use this recipe with traditional spareribs as well; just remember to purchase an extra pound or so.

PREP: 5 minutes   MARINATE: 8 hours or overnight
COOK: 2-1/2 hours

INGREDIENTS
    1 pound pork baby back ribs
    1 teaspoon ground cumin
    1 teaspoon chili powder
    1-1/2 teaspoon paprika
    1/4 teaspoon kosher salt
    1/4 teaspoon freshly ground pepper
    8-ounce bottle barbecue sauce

DIRECTIONS
1. Combine cumin, chili powder, paprika, salt and pepper in a small bowl. Rub the mixture over the ribs.

2.   Tear off 2 pieces of aluminum foil big enough to enclose ribs. Spray each piece of foil with vegetable cooking spray. Brush the ribs liberally with barbeque sauce and wrap tightly in the foil. Refrigerate for at least 8 hours, or overnight.

3. Preheat oven to 300°.

4. Bake ribs wrapped tightly in the foil for 2-1/2 hours. Remove from foil and add brush with more sauce, if desired.

5. Turn on broiler and cook until sauce is bubbly and caramelized, but not burned.

Serve with Corn on the Cob and Cole Slaw.

• SWEET AND SOUR SPARERIBS •

If you love the sweet and sour zing of Hawaiian cuisine, then this recipe is for you. Double it for company, they'll love you for it.

PREP: 10 minutes   COOK: 2 hours

INGREDIENTS
   2 tablespoons rice or white wine vinegar
   1/4 cup ketchup
   1-1/2 teaspoons soy sauce
   1/2 (8-ounce) can crushed pineapple, undrained
   1-1/2 tablespoons brown sugar
   1 tablespoon cornstarch
   1/4 teaspoon kosher salt
   3/4 teaspoon fresh ginger, grated or 1/2 teaspoon dried
   1-1/2 pounds pork spareribs, cut into serving size pieces

DIRECTIONS
   1. Preheat oven to 325°.

   2. Combine the vinegar, ketchup, soy sauce and pineapple in a small bowl. Add to a small sauce pan and heat over medium heat. Stir in the brown sugar, cornstarch, salt, and ginger. Cook, stirring constantly, until slightly thickened, about 5 minutes.

   3. Place a layer of spareribs in a 9x12 roasting pan. Pour half of the sauce over the top. Arrange another layer of spareribs, and top with remaining sauce. Cover tightly with tin foil.

   4. Bake ribs until they are done and falling off the bone, about 1-1/2 to 2 hours.

Serve with Garlic Smashed Potatoes and Orange Glazed Carrots.

Lamb

 Lamb

Why don't Americans eat more lamb? Got me. Sheep were originally domesticated in the Middle East and Asia more than 10,000 years ago and lamb is now one of the most abundant livestock in the world. Seems everybody in the world eats more lamb than we do. In Australia, New Zealand and Kuwait, the per capita consumption is 40 pounds. In Greece, it's 30 pounds and in England, Ireland and Spain - about 14. Here at home we eat less than a pound. Sheesh. If we'd only realize that lamb is as high as beef in protein, iron and B vitamins, but lower in fat, perhaps we would reconsider. Besides, lamb is absolutely delicious. Just try a few of the grilled lamb chop recipes that follow and you'll also wonder why we consume only one pound of lamb compared to 65 pounds of beef and 50 pounds of pork each year.

Perhaps it has something to do with the way lamb has been prepared in our past: tough, gray, and flavorless. Or maybe we were offered an overcooked gourmet version of chops slathered with some radioactive-looking green jelly. Here the world's great cuisines have something to teach us. Lamb should be cooked to medium rare and, like an excellent cut of prime beef, rarely requires more than a pinch of salt and a sprinkling of freshly ground pepper. But should you desire a sauce, the kitchens of the Middle East, India, China, and Australia have much to offer.

To be honest, certain cuts of lamb are expensive and should be reserved for special occasions. But many cuts fall within our everyday budgets and should be a part of our monthly menu. So head to the market and purchase a few chops or ribs and prepare them as described in the following pages. I guarantee your consumption of lamb will soon be well above the measly pound that most Americans eat, and your palate will be happier for it.

• HERB MARINATED LAMB CHOPS •

I've specified four lamb loin chops for this recipe but you may also substitute two shoulder chops; they're bigger and a little less expensive.

PREP: 10 Minutes   MARINATE: 2+ Hours
COOK: 15 Minutes

INGREDIENTS
    2 tablespoons dry red wine
    1 tablespoon soy sauce
    3/4 teaspoon minced fresh mint
    1/2 teaspoon minced fresh basil
    1/4 teaspoon freshly ground pepper
    1 garlic clove, peeled and minced
    4 lamb loin chops (1-inch thick)

DIRECTIONS
1. Combine the wine, soy sauce, mint, basil, pepper, and garlic in a small bowl. Place meat in a re-sealable plastic bag. Pour marinade over chops and refrigerate for at least 2 hours, turning occasionally.

2. Preheat an outdoor grill for medium-high heat, or preheat oven broiler.

3. Drain and discard marinade. Pat dry chops and grill to desired doneness, about 2 - 3 minutes per side for medium-rare, or broil in the oven about 4 minutes per side, until meat reaches desired doneness (for medium-rare, a meat thermometer should read 145°; for medium, 160°; well-done, 170°).

Serve with Brown Rice and Cashews and Broccoli Au Gratin.

• BISTRO LAMB CHOPS •

This traditional bistro dish will fill your home with a wonderful aroma. Don't open the windows or you'll find your neighbors leaning in and begging for a plate!

PREP: 10 minutes   COOK: 10 minutes

INGREDIENTS
   2 tablespoon olive oil, divided
   1 tablespoon Dijon mustard
   1 tablespoon balsamic vinegar
   1 teaspoon dried thyme
   1 garlic clove, peeled and minced
   1/8 teaspoon kosher salt
   1/8 teaspoon freshly ground pepper
   4 lamb loin chops (1-inch thick)
   1/2 medium sweet red pepper, thinly sliced
   1 small zucchini, thinly sliced
   1/2 medium onion (sweet if available), thinly sliced

DIRECTIONS
   1.   Preheat oven broiler.

   2.   Combine 1 tablespoon oil, mustard, vinegar, thyme, garlic, salt and pepper in a small bowl; reserve 1 teaspoon.

   3.   Spread mustard mixture over both sides of chops. Broil for 4-6 minutes on each side or until meat reaches desired doneness (for medium-rare, a meat thermometer should read 145°; medium, 160°; well-done, 170°).

   3.   Meanwhile, sauté the red pepper, zucchini and onion in remaining oil in a small skillet over medium-high heat until crisp-tender. Stir in reserved mustard mixture and toss to coat. Spoon over chops and serve.

Serve with Roasted Red Potatoes and a Crusty Loaf of French Bread.

• GRILLED LAMB CHOPS WITH BROWN SUGAR •

I love a thick, juicy steak, but these grilled lamb chops run a very close second. I particularly like the crisp, thin crust that the brown sugar provides as it caramelizes.

PREP: 15 minutes   MARINATE: 2 hours+
COOK: 10 minutes

INGREDIENTS
  2 tablespoons brown sugar
  1 teaspoon ground ginger
  1 teaspoon dried tarragon
  1/2 teaspoon ground cinnamon
  1/2 teaspoon ground black pepper
  1/2 teaspoon garlic powder
  1/4 teaspoon kosher salt
  4 lamb loin chops (1-inch thick)

DIRECTIONS
  1. Combine first 7 ingredients in a small bowl. Rub lamb chops with the mixture and place on a plate. Cover, and refrigerate for at least 2 hours.

  2. Preheat grill or broiler for high heat.

  3. Grill to desired doneness, about 3 minutes per side for medium or broil in the oven about 5 minutes per side for medium.

Serve with Buttered Noodles and Carrots in Vermouth.

• BAKED LAMB CHOPS •

I prefer grilled lamb chops but sometimes I need more time to prepare a side dish or dessert. Baking the chops gives me at least half an hour to do that.

PREP: 10 minutes   COOK: 45 minutes

INGREDIENTS
  1 egg
  2 teaspoons Worcestershire sauce
  4 lamb loin chops (1-inch thick)
  2/3 cup dry bread crumbs

DIRECTIONS
  1.   Preheat oven to 375°.

  2.   Combine the egg and the Worcestershire sauce in a small bowl. Dip each lamb chop in the sauce then lightly dredge in the bread crumbs. Shake off excess crumbs and arrange chops in a lightly oiled baking dish.

  3.   Bake for 20 minutes, turn chops over, and bake for 20 more minutes, or to desired doneness (for medium-rare, a meat thermometer should read 145° degrees; for medium, 160°; well-done, 170°).

Serve with Boiled New Potatoes and Sautéed Broccoli with Mustard Butter and Capers.

• BRAISED LAMB SHANKS •

Braised lamb shanks are a tried and true comfort food. Try this or any of the following braised dishes on a cold winter's night to warm your evening. Serve with warm bread and a good California Cabernet Sauvignon or Merlot.

PREP: 20 Minutes   COOK: 2 Hours

INGREDIENTS
    2 lamb shanks (1/2 pound each)
    2 teaspoons olive oil
    1/2 pound potatoes, peeled and diced
    1/2 pound carrots, peeled and diced
    1 onion, peeled and diced
    2 tablespoons all-purpose flour
    2 tablespoons unsalted butter, melted

DIRECTIONS
1. Heat oil in a small Dutch oven over medium-high heat. Add shanks and cook, turning to brown all sides, about 12-15 minutes. Add water to cover, reduce heat to low and simmer for about 1 hour.

2. Add potatoes, carrots and onions and simmer for about 1 hour.

3. In a small bowl, whisk flour into melted butter to make a roux, then stir into simmering dish to thicken.

• BRAISED LAMB SHANKS IN RED WINE SAUCE •

Most of the recipes in this book can be prepared in under an hour. This is not one of them. However, the prep time is minimal, and once the dish is in the oven you will have 3 hours to concentrate on other things, like making that creme dessert you saw in the glossy magazine. You know the one: Seventeen ingredients and forty-two steps. Or not.

PREP: 20 Minutes   COOK: 3 Hours

INGREDIENTS

1 large onion, chopped
2 lamb shanks (1/2 pound each)
1 cup dry red wine
1/2 cup balsamic vinegar
1/2 teaspoon dried oregano
3 tablespoons olive oil
2 cloves garlic, pressed
1 lemon, quartered

1 (15-ounce) can diced tomatoes, with juice
1 tablespoon chopped fresh basil or 1-1/2 teaspoons dried
1-1/2 teaspoons kosher salt
1-1/2 teaspoons cracked black pepper

DIRECTIONS

1. Preheat the oven to 350°.

2. Place the onions in a layer in the bottom of a small Dutch oven. Arrange the lamb shanks on top of the onions.

3. Combine the wine, balsamic vinegar, oregano, olive oil, and garlic in a small bowl. Pour over the lamb and place a quarter of a lemon on each side of the shanks. Pour the tomatoes over the lamb and season with basil, salt and pepper.

4. Cover and cook for 3 hours.

5. Remove shanks to a warm plate and cover. Place Dutch oven on a stove over medium high heat and reduce sauce. Spoon over shanks and serve.

Note: If you don't want to heat up the oven, you can simmer this dish on the stove top instead.

Serve with Parmesan Noodles and Sautéed Summer Squash or Zucchini.

• BRAISED LAMB SHANKS IN WHITE WINE SAUCE •

This stovetop version renders a slightly sweeter sauce because the onions are sautéed prior to simmering.

PREP: 10 minutes   COOK: 2 Hours 50 minutes

INGREDIENTS
 1-1/2 tablespoons olive oil
 2 lamb shanks (1/2 pound each)
 1/2 small onion, chopped
 3 cloves garlic, sliced
 1 teaspoon chopped fresh rosemary or 1/2 teaspoon dried
 Salt and freshly ground black pepper taste
 1/2 cup dry white wine
 Rosemary sprigs for garnish

DIRECTIONS

1. Heat oil in a small Dutch oven over medium-high heat. Add shanks and cook, turning to brown all sides, about 12-15 minutes. Transfer to a plate.

2. Reduce heat to medium-low. Add the onion and sauté until translucent, about 8 minutes. Add garlic and sauté 1 additional minute.

3. Return shanks to the pan. Season with rosemary and salt and pepper to taste. Pour in wine, raise heat to medium-high and bring to a boil. Reduce heat to low, cover tightly, and simmer until the shanks are very tender, 2 to 2 1/2 hours. Turn once or twice during cooking and add water as necessary to maintain original level of liquid. Garnish with rosemary sprigs.

Serve with Boiled New Potatoes and Green Beans Amandine.

• IRISH STEW •

This may indeed be the ultimate in comfort food. Note the two different ways the potatoes are prepared; this adds a nice texture and nuance to the dish. Traditionally, Irish stew is made with lamb, but you can make this with beef if you prefer. I've made the recipe for four because it'll taste even better the next day.

PREP: 25 minutes   COOK: 2 hours

INGREDIENTS
1-1/2 pounds boneless lamb shoulder, cubed
1 tablespoon olive oil
2 medium onions, halved and sliced
2 celery stalks, sliced
2 medium new or all purpose potatoes, peeled and sliced
1/2 teaspoon thyme
2 tablespoons chopped fresh parsley
1/2 teaspoon Worcestershire sauce
3 cups beef stock
3 medium new or all purpose potatoes, cut in large cubes
4 carrots, peeled and sliced
Salt and pepper to taste

DIRECTIONS
1. Preheat oven to 325°.

2. Heat olive oil in a Dutch oven over medium-high heat. Add onion and celery and sauté until soft, about 8 minutes.

3. Add the lamb meat, sliced potatoes, thyme, parsley, and Worcestershire sauce. Pour in the beef stock and add cubed potatoes, pushing them down into the stew.

4. Cover and bake for 1 hour. Add the carrots and cook for an additional hour until vegetables and meat are very tender. Add salt and pepper to taste. Divide into bowls and garnish with additional parsley.

• LAMB CURRY •

This dish is prepared with a simple homemade curry powder, but you may also use a good store-bought curry powder.

PREP: 10 minutes   COOK: 1 hour 15 minutes

INGREDIENTS
   1/4 cup olive oil
   4 medium onions, chopped
   1 garlic clove, peeled and minced
   1-1/2 pounds boneless lamb shoulder, cut into 2-inch cubes
   1/2 cup dry white wine
   1 cup plain yogurt
   1/2 teaspoon sugar

Curry:
   2 teaspoons ground coriander
   1 teaspoon ground ginger
   1/2 teaspoon ground cardamom
   1/4 teaspoon ground cloves
   1/4 teaspoon ground cinnamon
   Salt and pepper to taste

DIRECTIONS

1. Heat the oil in a Dutch oven over medium-high heat. Add the onions and sauté until soft and translucent, about 8 minutes. Add the garlic and sauté for 1 additional minute. Remove onions and garlic to a small bowl.

2. Add the lamb and brown on all sides (you may have to do this in batches). Add the wine and deglaze the pot, scraping up any brown bits on the bottom.

3. Return the onions and garlic to the pot and add the yogurt, sugar and curry spice. Reduce heat to low then cover and simmer for about 1 hour until meat is tender.

Serve with Steamed White Rice and Steamed Peas.

• RACK OF LAMB, CANNES STYLE •

This wonderful recipe is from Jack Ubaldi who ran the Florence Prime Meat Market in Greenwich Village for forty years before 'retiring' to teach in the Culinary Arts Program at the New School. Although out of print, *Jack Ubaldi's Meat Book, A Butcher's Guide to Buying, Cutting and Cooking Meat* is filled with lots of information, wonderful stories, and mouth-watering recipes. This book is well-worth searching out. When Mr. Ubaldi passed away in July of 2001 at the age of 90, the culinary universe lost a shining star.

PREP: 10 minutes   COOK: 45 minutes

INGREDIENTS

2 anchovy filets, chopped
1 tablespoon capers, chopped
2 tablespoons bread crumbs
2 garlic cloves, peeled and chopped
1/2 teaspoon hot pepper sauce
1 tablespoon chopped fresh parsley
1 teaspoon fresh rosemary, or 1/2 teaspoon dried

salt and pepper to taste
olive oil to make a paste
1 rack of lamb, trimmed and
   frenched
1 tablespoon honey

DIRECTIONS

1. Preheat oven to 425°.

2. In a small bowl, mix the anchovies, capers, breadcrumbs, garlic, Hot pepper sauce, parsley, rosemary, salt and pepper with just enough olive oil to make a paste. Spread the mixture over the meat side of the rack of lamb. Cover the ends of the bones with foil to prevent charring.

3. Place the rack in a baking pan and roast for 45 minutes.

4. Remove the pan from the oven and spread the honey over the lamb. Turn on broiler and return the pan to the oven for a final 2 or 3 minutes.

Serve with Boiled New Potatoes and Grilled Tomatoes with Garlic and Rosemary.

Vegetarian

 ## VEGETARIAN

Vegetarian meals can, and should be, part of a healthy diet. Studies by the American Dietetic Association found that a properly planned vegetarian diet satisfies the nutritional needs for all stages of life and may significantly lower the risk of cancer and heart disease. For many people in the world, vegetarianism (or something very like it) is the only diet they know because of their economic circumstances. Simply put, meat costs more than beans, grains, and vegetables. As a result, meat is usually served on special occasions if it's served at all. And even where meat is plentiful, many still eat it in moderation - often as a side dish - while vegetables and grains take center stage. Speaking as a tried and true omnivore, adding vegetarian meals to our diets and cutting back on animal protein is not only good for us, but also good for the earth (and that, my friend, is a whole 'nother book).

Fortunately, the cuisines of the world offer a magnificent array of vegetarian meals and I've included a small sampling of them here. Gone are the bland vegetarian stereotypes that many of us hold in our minds. But to be honest, some of those stereotypes are justified. My first intentional vegetarian meal experience (I say 'intentional' because my mom often made vegetarian meals – i.e. her incredible pasta and sauce - she just didn't call these meals vegetarian) was the result of a third grade lunch-swap gone bad. I traded a perfectly delicious BLT for my friend's lunch: a pile of wilted sprouts sandwiched between two slices of un-chewable bread and slathered with an industrial-green mystery sauce. He lured me into it with a bet. "Man, I don't think you never tasted anything like this before." He was right.

In the pages that follow, I offer an array of savory and easy to prepare vegetarian dishes. And not a one consists of wilted sprouts, stale bread and industrial green mystery sauce.

• FRIED TEMPEH •

Tempeh is a high-protein, cholesterol-free, low-fat soybean cake that's often used as a meat substitute. You'll find it in most natural food stores and many supermarkets.

PREP: 5 minutes   MARINATE: 20 minutes
COOK: 10 minutes

INGREDIENTS
- 1 clove crushed garlic
- 1/2 cup water
- 1/4 teaspoon kosher salt, or to taste
- 1 (8-ounce) package tempeh
- 1/2 cup olive or canola oil

DIRECTIONS

1. Combine the garlic, water, and salt in a small bowl. Stir to mix well.

2. Slice the tempeh 1-inch thick and score both sides. Marinate in the garlic mixture for 20 minutes.

3. Heat oil over medium-high heat in a 10-inch skillet. Pan-fry the tempeh until brown on both sides.

Serve with Steamed White Rice and your choice of dipping sauce: soy, barbeque, honey mustard, etc.

• VEGETARIAN PAD THAI •

Pad Thai is probably the most popular menu item in Thai restaurants across America. While it usually includes shrimp or chicken, this vegetarian version will surely appeal to anyone who enjoys this spicy noodle dish.

PREP: 1 hour   COOK: 20 minutes

INGREDIENTS

1/4 pound dried rice noodles
2 teaspoons olive oil, divided
1 egg, beaten
1-1/2 teaspoons peanut oil
1/4 cup and 2 tablespoons peanut butter
1 tablespoon water
1-1/2 tablespoons soy sauce
1/4 cup milk
1/4 cup plus 1 tablespoon brown sugar
1 tablespoon lemon juice
1-1/2 teaspoons garlic powder
3/4 teaspoon paprika

cayenne pepper to taste
4 ounces bean sprouts
1/4 cup shredded carrots
1 tablespoon chopped
   green onions
2 tablespoons chopped, unsalted
   dry-roasted peanuts
1/2 lime, cut into wedges

DIRECTIONS

1.   Submerge the rice noodles in a bowl of hot water for about an hour (noodles should be very flexible, but still relatively firm).

2.   Heat 1 teaspoon olive oil in a 10-inch skillet over medium heat. Add egg and scramble. Transfer to plate and set aside.

3.   In a medium saucepan, combine the peanut oil, peanut butter, water, soy sauce, milk, brown sugar, and lemon juice. Season with garlic powder and paprika. Heat and stir until sauce is smooth. Season liberally with cayenne pepper.

4.   Drain noodles. Heat remaining olive oil in a medium skillet over medium heat. Add noodles and cook, stirring constantly, until they are tender, about 2 minutes.

5.   Stir in peanut sauce, sprouts, carrots, scallions, ground peanuts, and the scrambled eggs. Continue to cook over medium heat until vegetables are crisp-tender, about 5 minutes. Serve immediately, garnished with lime.

• SOUTHWESTERN VEGETARIAN PASTA •

I like to double the sauce of this recipe. I'll use half on the pasta and then add a cup of vegetable broth to the remaining sauce to create a hearty soup for lunch the next day.

PREP: 10 minutes   COOK: 20 minutes

INGREDIENTS
   1-1/2 teaspoons olive oil
   1/2 onion, chopped
   1/2 green bell pepper, diced
   1 clove garlic, chopped
   1 tablespoon chili powder
   1/2 teaspoon ground cumin
   1 (14.5-ounce) can diced tomatoes with juice
   1/2 (15-ounce) can chickpeas, drained
   1/2 (10-ounce) package frozen corn kernels, thawed
   6 ounces uncooked elbow macaroni
   1/4 cup shredded Monterey Jack cheese

DIRECTIONS
   1.   Heat oil in a 10-inch skillet over medium-high heat. Sauté onion, green pepper, garlic, chili powder, and cumin until onion is soft and translucent, about 8 minutes.

   2.   Stir in tomatoes, chickpeas, and corn. Reduce heat to low and simmer 15 to 20 minutes, or until thickened and heated through.

   3.   Meanwhile, bring a pot of lightly salted water to a boil. Add macaroni and cook for 8 to 10 minutes or until al dente; drain.

   4.   Combine pasta and sauce. Sprinkle each serving with Monterey Jack cheese.

• VEGETARIAN CHILI •

What's chili without meat? This. And it's darned good!

PREP: 10 minutes   COOK: 30 minutes

INGREDIENTS
- 1 tablespoon extra-virgin olive oil
- 1 cup chopped red onion
- 4 cloves garlic, crushed
- 1 tablespoon chili powder or more to taste
- 1-1/2 teaspoons ground cumin
- 1 (14.5-ounce) can diced tomatoes
- 1 (15-ounce) can black beans, drained
- 2/3 cup vegetable broth or white wine
- 1 red or yellow bell pepper, chopped
- 1 cup chopped zucchini
- 1 cup frozen corn kernels
- 1 cup chopped white or Portobello mushrooms
- 2/3 cup chopped fresh cilantro, packed
- 1/8 teaspoon cayenne pepper, or more to taste
- Salt and freshly ground black pepper to taste

DIRECTIONS
1. Heat oil in medium Dutch oven over medium heat. Add onion, chili powder and cumin. Sauté over medium heat until onion is soft and translucent, about 10 minutes. Add garlic and sauté 1 minute.

2. Stir in remaining ingredients and bring to a boil. Lower heat and simmer 20 minutes or until vegetables are soft. Add more liquid if needed.

Serve over Steamed White Rice and garnish with any of the following: grated cheddar cheese, chopped onion, sour cream or guacamole.

• SCALLOPED TOMATOES •

This is an ideal main dish for a light summer meal. But it also makes an excellent side dish. Just reduce the ingredients.

PREP: 5 minutes   COOK: 35 minutes

INGREDIENTS
  2 tablespoons unsalted butter
  1/2 onion, chopped
  1 clove garlic, crushed
  1/2 teaspoon kosher salt
  Ground black pepper to taste
  1/4 teaspoon dried basil
  2 teaspoons brown sugar
  2 or 3 tomatoes, sliced
  1/2 cup seasoned Italian bread crumbs
  1/4 cup grated Parmesan cheese

DIRECTIONS
  1.   Preheat oven to 375°.

  2.   Melt butter in a small saucepan over medium heat. Add onion and sauté until onion is soft and translucent, about 10 minutes. Add garlic and sauté 1 additional minute. Stir in salt, pepper, basil, brown sugar and tomatoes. Add bread crumbs and stir until all of the ingredients are well seasoned.

  3.   Pour the tomato bread mixture into a greased casserole dish and sprinkle with cheese. Bake for 30 to 35 minutes.

• VEGETARIAN KORMA •

This is an easy and exotic southern Indian dish. It's rich, creamy, and extremely flavorful. Traditionally, it's a fairly mild curry, but you can leave the seeds in the jalapeno peppers for a tad more heat.

PREP: 10 minutes   COOK: 30 minutes

INGREDIENTS
   1 tablespoon olive oil
   1 small onion, diced
   1/2 teaspoon minced fresh ginger
   2 cloves garlic, minced
   1 red potato, peeled and cubed
   2 carrots, cubed
   1 small fresh jalapeno pepper, seeded and sliced
   1-1/2 tablespoons ground unsalted cashews
   1-1/2 tablespoons raisins
   1/2 (4-ounce) can tomato sauce
   1 teaspoon kosher salt
   1 tablespoon curry powder
   1/2 cup frozen green peas
   1/2 red bell pepper, chopped
   1/2 cup coconut milk
   Fresh cilantro for garnish

DIRECTIONS
   1.   Heat the oil in a 10-inch skillet over medium heat. Add the onion and sauté until soft and translucent, about 10 minutes. Add ginger and garlic and sauté 1 additional minute. Add potatoes, carrots, jalapeno, cashews, raisins and tomato sauce then season with salt and curry powder. Cook, stirring, for 10 minutes, or until potatoes are tender.

   2.   Stir in peas, red bell pepper, and coconut milk. Reduce heat to low, cover, and simmer 10 minutes. Garnish with cilantro.

Serve over steamed white rice.

• MALAYSIAN QUINOA •

Quinoa (pronounced keen-wa) was a staple of the Incas. They called it the mother grain. They were right. One cup of cooked quinoa has more calcium than a quart of milk, and ounce for ounce has as much protein as meat. It contains all essential amino acids and has high amounts of magnesium and iron.

PREP: 5 minutes   COOK: 15 minutes

INGREDIENTS
  1-1/2 cups water or vegetable broth, divided
  1/2 cup textured vegetable protein (TVP)
  1 tablespoon peanut butter
  1 tablespoon canned cream of coconut
  1/2 Thai birds eye chili, seeded and minced (or 1/2 scotch bonnet or
      habanero pepper to taste)
  1 green onion, chopped
  1 teaspoon chopped cilantro
  1/2 cup uncooked quinoa
  Salt and pepper to taste

DIRECTIONS
  1. Boil 1/2 cup water or broth in a small saucepan and pour into a bowl. Stir in the TVP and let sit for a minute or two. Blend in peanut butter, cream of coconut, chili, green onion and cilantro. Cover and keep warm while the quinoa cooks.

  2. Bring quinoa and remaining 1 cup water to a boil in a small saucepan. Reduce heat to low, cover, and simmer 15 minutes until quinoa is fluffy. Stir in the TVP and peanut butter sauce and season with salt and pepper to serve.

• STUFFED GREEN PEPPERS •

I remember eating incredible stuffed green peppers at a dive called - get this - The Stuffed Pepper. Aside from a wide assortment of alcohol-infused libations, this was the only item on the menu. No wonder they referred to their establishment as the 'attitude adjustment emporium'. This is a healthier version of that classic American diner dish.

PREP: 10 minutes   COOK: 1 hour

INGREDIENTS
  1/2 cup uncooked white rice
  1 cup water
  1/2 (15-ounce) can black beans, drained and rinsed
  1-1/2 teaspoons chili powder
  2 green bell peppers
  8 slices Swiss or Provolone cheese
  1 (8-ounce) can tomato sauce

DIRECTIONS
  1. Preheat oven to 400°.

  2. Bring water to a boil In a small saucepan. Add rice and stir. Reduce heat, cover and simmer for 20 minutes.

  3. Combine cooked rice with black beans and chili powder. Cut the tops off of the peppers and remove the ribs and seeds. Spoon about 2 tablespoons of the rice and bean mixture into the bottoms of the peppers. Lay a slice of cheese on top and repeat 3 more times, ending with cheese on top.

  4. Bake until peppers soften, about 45 minutes.

  5. Meanwhile, heat tomato sauce in a small saucepan over low to medium heat. Slice peppers in half, top with tomato sauce and serve.

• PORTOBELLO MUSHROOM BURGERS •

It's hard to imagine that these large fungi were once despised by growers. They threw them out or took them home, but in the late 1980's something happened. Through clever marketing the lowly Portobello, and its little brother, the cremini, became extremely desirable. Go figure. Because the Portobello is circular, flat, and the size of a regular hamburger, it's perfect for this backyard party favorite. In fact, many find their meaty taste and dense, chewy texture on a par with, or even superior to, beef. Portobellos, as you'll find from this recipe, are excellent for grilling or roasting.

PREP: 15 minutes   COOK: 15 minutes

INGREDIENTS
   2 Portobello mushroom caps
   2 tablespoons balsamic vinegar
   1 tablespoon extra-virgin olive oil
   1/2 teaspoon dried basil
   1/2 teaspoon dried oregano
   1-1/2 teaspoons minced garlic
   Salt and pepper to taste
   2 slices provolone cheese

DIRECTIONS
1.   Place the mushroom caps, smooth side up, in a shallow dish. Whisk the vinegar, oil, basil, oregano, garlic, salt, and pepper together in a small bowl. Pour over the mushrooms. Let stand at room temperature for 15 minutes or so, turning twice.

2.   Preheat grill or broiler.

3.   Place mushrooms on the grill, reserving marinade for basting. Grill for 5 to 8 minutes per side, or until tender. Brush with marinade frequently. Top with cheese during the last 2 minutes of grilling.

Serve on a bun with lettuce, tomato and aioli sauce.

• SWEET POTATO BURRITOS •

I'm a sucker for bean burritos. Whoever came up with the idea of adding sweet potatoes deserves some kind of commemoration. Or at least one of those free bottomless bowl of chips and a side of salsa.

PREP: 5 minutes   COOK: 20 minutes

INGREDIENTS
  1 teaspoon olive oil
  1/2 onion, chopped
  1 clove garlic, minced
  2 cups canned kidney beans, drained
  2/3 cup water or vegetable broth
  1 tablespoon chili powder
  3/4 teaspoon ground cumin
  1-1/4 teaspoons prepared mustard
  Pinch cayenne pepper, or to taste
  1 tablespoon soy sauce
  1-1/3 cups cooked and mashed sweet potatoes (canned is fine)
  4 (10-inch) flour tortillas, warmed
  1/2 cup dice tomatoes
  6 tablespoons shredded Cheddar cheese

DIRECTIONS
  1. Preheat oven to 350°.

  2. Heat oil in a 10-inch skillet over medium-high heat and sauté onion until soft and translucent, about 8 minutes. Add garlic and sauté 1 additional minute. Stir in beans and mash. Gradually stir in water or broth and heat until warm. Remove from heat and stir in the chili powder, cumin, mustard, cayenne pepper, and soy sauce.

  3. Divide bean mixture and mashed sweet potatoes evenly between the warm flour tortillas. Top with tomatoes and cheese. Fold the tortillas 'burrito style' and place on a baking sheet.

  4. Bake for 12 minutes and serve.

Serve with sour cream, chopped green onions, salsa, and black beans.

• CHICKPEA CURRY •

PREP: 10 minutes   COOK: 1 hour 15 minutes

INGREDIENTS
   2 cups vegetable broth
   1/2 cup raisins
   2 tablespoons olive oil
   1 onion, chopped
   2 cloves garlic, minced
   1 tablespoon minced ginger
   1 cinnamon stick
   3 whole cloves
   1/2 teaspoon cayenne pepper
   1/2 teaspoon ground turmeric
   1/2 teaspoon ground coriander
   1/2 teaspoon ground cumin
   1 (19-ounce) chickpeas, drained
   1 small sweet potato, peeled and diced
   1 small pear, peeled and cubed
   Salt to taste
   1/2 cup chopped fresh cilantro

DIRECTIONS
   1. Place water or broth and raisins in a small saucepan over high heat.
       Bring to a boil, reduce heat and simmer for a few minutes.

   2. Meanwhile, heat olive oil in a medium saucepan over medium heat.
       Add onion, garlic, and ginger; cook and stir until the onion has
       softened and turned translucent, about 5 minutes. Add cinnamon
       stick, cloves, cayenne, turmeric, coriander and cumin; cook, stirring
       constantly, for about 3 minutes until fragrant.

   3. Stir in chickpeas, sweet potato and pear then pour in hot vegetable
       stock and raisins. Bring to a simmer then reduce heat to medium-low.
       Cover, and simmer until vegetables have softened and the sauce has
       thickened, about 1 hour.

   4. Season to taste with salt and stir in chopped cilantro before serving.

Serve with Steamed White Rice

• VEGETABLE BIRYANI •

This world-renowned Indian dish is usually made with layers of lamb or chicken. While those versions require lots of time (and practice) to make, this one can be put together in around half an hour.

PREP: 10 minutes   COOK: 20 minutes

INGREDIENTS
   1/2 cup Basmati rice
   2 teaspoons olive oil
   1/4 teaspoon cumin seeds
   2 whole cloves
   1/2 onion, chopped
   1-1/2 cups water or vegetable broth
   3/4 teaspoon kosher salt, or to taste
   1 tablespoon garam masala
   1/2 teaspoon chili powder, or to taste
   1/2 cup frozen mixed vegetables
   2 teaspoons unsalted butter

DIRECTIONS
   1.   Rinse and soak rice for 30 minutes; drain.

   2.   Heat oil in a large saucepan over medium heat. Sauté cumin seeds and cloves for about 1 minute. Add onion and sauté, stirring constantly, until soft and translucent, about 10 minutes. Stir in rice and sauté for about 1 minute.

   3.   Stir in the water or broth, salt, garam masala, chili powder and vegetables. Bring to a boil then reduce heat to low. Cover and simmer for 20 minutes, or until all water is absorbed. Fluff with a fork and stir in butter before serving.

• PORTOBELLO MUSHROOM STEW •

This is a delightful and filling winter stew. I like using a variety of mushrooms for added texture and flavor.

PREP: 10 minutes   COOK: 35 minutes

INGREDIENTS
- 1/4 cup olive oil, divided
- 1 large onion, diced
- 2 teaspoons chopped rosemary
- Salt and pepper to taste
- 1/8 teaspoon red pepper flakes, or more to taste
- 1/2 pound Portobello mushrooms, sliced 3/8 inches thick (remove gills)
- 1 pound large white or cremini mushrooms (or a combination of these and other varieties like chanterelle or shitake)
- 2 cloves garlic, minced
- 3 tablespoons tomato paste
- 1-1/2 cups vegetable broth
- 1 teaspoon white wine vinegar
- 2 tablespoons unsalted butter
- 2 tablespoons chopped fresh parsley

DIRECTIONS
1. Heat 1 tablespoon olive oil in a medium Dutch oven over medium heat. Add the onion and rosemary and sauté until soft and translucent, about 10 minutes. Season with salt, pepper, and red pepper flakes to taste then remove to a bowl.

2. Add 1 tablespoon olive oil to the pot and heat. Add the Portobello mushrooms and sauté until nicely brown, about 5 minutes. Remove them to the bowl and add the remaining olive oil to the skillet. Stir in the white mushrooms and sauté for about 5 minutes.

3. Return everything to the pot and add the garlic, tomato paste, broth, and vinegar. Reduce heat and simmer uncovered, for 12 to 15 minutes. Swirl in the butter to melt and add the parsley.

• SUMMER STEW WITH HERBED BUTTER •

Not all stews are made in the winter. Here's a light and bright stew that's brimming with fresh, colorful vegetables. Toss in a few sliced mushrooms for added depth.

PREP: 15 minutes   COOK: 30 minutes

INGREDIENTS
    4 tablespoons unsalted butter, softened
    1-1/2 tablespoons fresh chopped marjoram
    1-1/2 tablespoons chopped fresh basil
    1-1/2 tablespoons chopped fresh parsley
    1/2 teaspoon lemon zest
    Salt and pepper to taste
    1/2 pound green beans, cut in 2" pieces
    1 tablespoon olive oil
    1 medium onion, diced
    1 clove garlic, chopped
    1/2 cup vegetable broth
    1/2 pound yellow squash, diced
    1 red or yellow bell pepper, diced
    1 large ripe tomato, peeled, and diced
    3 cups fresh or frozen corn kernels
    1/2 teaspoon kosher salt
    Additional ground black pepper to taste

DIRECTIONS
1. Combine the butter, herbs, lemon zest, salt, and pepper in a small bowl.

2. Bring a pot of salted water to boil and add the beans. Parboil for 2 minutes and drain.

3. Heat the oil in a Dutch oven over medium-high heat. Add the onions and sauté until soft and translucent, about 8 minutes. Add the garlic and sauté 1 additional minute.

4. Add the broth, reduce heat to low, and simmer, covered, for 5 minutes. Add the green beans, squash, bell pepper, tomato and corn. Season with salt and simmer for 10 minutes or until vegetables are tender. Add herb butter and stir. Season with additional salt and pepper to taste.

Sides

BASIC VEGGIES
• ASPARAGUS •

This wonderful spring vegetable can be found in a variety of colors: green, purple, green and purple, and creamy white. Choose thin stalks - they tend to be younger, and therefore, more tender.

Asparagus has been cultivated and cooked from ancient times and is a good source of folic acid, potassium and dietary fiber.

Many folks coat their asparagus with thick sauces like Hollandaise, but in my book, asparagus needs very little in the ways of seasoning. Simply sprinkle the cooked spears with a little kosher salt and pepper, then drizzle with butter or olive oil and sprinkle with grated Parmesan, pecorino or white cheddar cheese.

To Boil: In a small or medium skillet, bring 5 cups of water to a boil and add 2-1/2 teaspoons salt. Add 1/2 pound asparagus in one layer and return to a boil. Cook uncovered until crisp-tender.

- 4 – 5 minutes for thin spears
- 6 – 7 minutes for medium spears
- 8 - 9 minutes for thick spears

To Steam: Place 1/2 pound asparagus spears in a steamer basket over an inch or two of boiling water. Cover and steam.

- 4 – 5 minutes for thin spears
- 6 – 7 minutes for medium spears
- 8 - 9 minutes for thick spears

To Microwave: Place 1/2 pound asparagus in a microwave baking dish. Add 1 tablespoon chicken stock, wine, or water; cover and cook on high for 4 –9 minutes, stirring halfway through, until crisp-tender. Remove and let stand for 2 additional minutes.

To Roast: Wash and pat dry asparagus and brush liberally with olive oil or butter. Grill over a medium charcoal fire until crisp-tender.

To Sauté: Melt 1-1/2 teaspoons butter and 1-1/2 tablespoon olive oil in a 10-inch skillet over medium heat. Add asparagus and sauté, stirring often until crisp-tender, about 10 minutes. Sprinkle with your choice of sharp cheese.

• BROCCOLI •

This is one of the green cruciferous vegetables that we refused to eat as children, the other being Brussels sprouts. I think the reason was because these, along with most vegetables, were cooked and cooked until they turned into mush. Think school cafeterias, greasy-spoon diners, or all-you-can-eat buffets. But it was to our loss. The American Cancer Society announced years ago that we could reduce our risk of some cancers if we simply added broccoli and other cruciferous vegetables to our diet. Still not convinced? The recipes below will change your view of this nutritious vegetable.

To Boil: In a saucepan, bring 8 cups of water to a boil and add 2-1/2 teaspoons kosher salt. Add 1/2 pound broccoli and return to a boil. Cook uncovered until crisp-tender.

- 2 – 4 minutes for florets
- 6 – 8 minutes for stalks

To Steam: Place 1/2 pound florets or tender stalks in a steamer basket over an inch or two of boiling water. Cover and steam.

- 5 or so minutes for florets
- 10 minutes for stalks

To Microwave: Place 1/2 pound broccoli in a microwave baking dish. If using stalks, arrange in a circle with stalks pointing toward the center. Add 1 tablespoon chicken stock, wine, or water; cover and cook on high for 5 – 8 minutes, stirring halfway through, until crisp-tender. Remove and let stand for 2 additional minutes.

• BRUSSELS SPROUTS •

Brussels sprouts are basically small cabbages. They are among the same family that includes broccoli and cauliflower. Although it contains a good amount of vitamin A, vitamin C, folic acid and dietary fiber, the lowly Brussels sprout was despised by most of us when we were young. Hopefully, the recipes that follow will win you over.

To Prepare: Cut a small x in the bottom of each spout to help them cook quickly.

To Boil: In a saucepan, bring 8 cups of water to a boil and add 2-1/2 teaspoons kosher salt. Add 1/2 pound Brussels sprouts and return to a boil. Cook uncovered until crisp-tender, about 6 - 12 minutes.

To Steam: Place 1/2 pound Brussels sprouts in a steamer basket over an inch or two of boiling water. Cover and steam for 8-15 minutes until crisp-tender.

To Microwave: Place 1/2 pound Brussels sprouts in a microwave-safe baking dish. Add 2 tablespoons chicken stock, wine, or water; cover and cook on high for 6-8 minutes, stirring halfway through, until crisp-tender. Remove and let stand for 3 additional minutes.

Brussels sprouts are excellent with butter and lemon-pepper, Parmesan cheese, toasted breadcrumbs or cheese sauce – many of the same recipes for broccoli.

• CARROTS •

This versatile root vegetable is a great source of dietary fiber, antioxidants and minerals. Delicious raw or cooked, carrots can be found in beverages, salads, soups, main courses, and even desserts.

Dill, parsley, thyme, mint, chervil, ginger, and nutmeg are great additions to carrots as are brown sugar, honey, raisins, oranges, tangerines, and lemons.

Cooked carrots taste great with just a little butter, kosher salt, and pepper. But feel free to experiment with the herbs and spices above.

To Boil: In a saucepan, bring 8 cups of water to a boil and add 2-1/2 teaspoons kosher salt. Add 1/2 pound carrots and return to a boil. Cook uncovered.

- 5 minutes or so for sliced, diced or matchstick cuts
- 8 minutes or so for halved (length-wise) cuts
- 12-15 minutes for whole carrots

To Steam: Place 1/2 pound carrots in a steamer basket over an inch or two of boiling water. Cover and steam.

- 8 minutes for sliced, diced or matchstick cuts
- 16 – 20 minutes for halved or whole carrots

To Microwave: Place 1/2 pound carrots in a microwave baking dish. Add 1 tablespoon chicken stock, wine, or water; cover and cook on high for 5 – 8 minutes, stirring halfway through, until crisp-tender. Remove and let stand for 3 additional minutes.

• CAULIFLOWER •

Though milder in flavor than broccoli, this sister cruciferous vegetable is low in fat and high in dietary fiber, folic acid, and vitamin C.

Cauliflower may be enjoyed with a cheese sauce, toasted almonds, curry powder, nutmeg or mace.

Note: Cauliflower may be substituted for any of the following broccoli recipes.

To Prepare: Cut the head in half or quarters and cut out the tough core. Break the florets into the desired size.

To Boil: In a saucepan, bring 8 cups of water to a boil and add 2-1/2 teaspoons kosher salt and 1-1/2 tablespoons lemon juice. Add 1/2 pound cauliflower and return to a boil. Cook uncovered until crisp-tender, about 3-5 minutes.

To Steam: Place 1/2 pound cauliflower in a steamer basket over an inch or two of boiling water. Cover and steam for 6-8 minutes until crisp-tender.

To Microwave: Place 1/2 pound cauliflower in a microwave baking dish. If using stalks, arrange in a circle with stalks pointing toward the center. Add 1 tablespoon chicken stock, wine, or water; cover and cook on high for 3 – 5 minutes, stirring halfway through, until crisp-tender. Remove and let stand for 2 additional minutes.

• CORN •

Corn is truly one of the simplest side dishes to prepare. I'm always amazed when I see folks boil it until it nearly turns to mush. Corn doesn't really need to be cooked, it just needs to be 'threatened' - The following methods will show you how. Simply add some sweet cream butter and a little salt and pepper for a delightful summertime treat Thanks to our growers in Florida, corn is now available year-round.

To Boil: In a kettle, bring enough water to a boil so that the corn will be covered. Add 1 tablespoon kosher salt for each quart of water. Remove the corn husks and trim the ends (optional). Drop the corn into the boiling water and return to a boil. Immediately turn off the heat and allow the corn to stand for exactly 5 minutes.

To Steam: Place shucked corn in a pot with 1 to 2 inches of boiling salted water. Cover and steam until corn is heated through, about 5 to 10 minutes.

To Grill or Roast: Start a charcoal fire, preheat a gas grill, or preheat an oven to 450°. Peel the corn husks back and remove the silk. Replace husks and grill for 15-20 minutes or roast 20-30 minutes in the oven.

To Sauté: In a small skillet, heat 1 tablespoon olive oil over medium heat. Add 1-1/2 cups corn and sauté for 3-4 minutes.

Variations: Add 1/4 cup of either chopped tomato, red or green bell pepper, onion or lima beans and sauté with the corn.

• GREEN BEANS •

Fresh green beans do not require a lot of preparation – simply rinse and cook. It's that simple. You may trim the ends if that suits your fancy; I prefer them without the strings. Frozen green beans work well in all of these recipes, but as with most vegetables, avoid canned.

Cooked green beans with a touch of butter, kosher salt and pepper would go well with most of the entrees in this book. A pinch of dill, chervil, parsley or mint to taste will make a wonderful addition to this easy to prepare vegetable.

To Boil: In a saucepan, bring 6 cups of water to a boil and add 2-1/2 teaspoons kosher salt. Add 1/2 pound green beans and return to a boil. Cook uncovered until crisp-tender, about 2 – 4 minutes for French style and 4-8 minutes for whole beans, until crisp-tender.

To Steam: Place 1/2 pound green beans in a steamer basket over an inch or two of boiling water. Cover and steam for 5-7 minutes for French style and 8-12 minutes for whole beans until crisp-tender.

To Microwave: Place 1/2 pound green beans in a microwave baking dish Add 2 tablespoon chicken stock, wine, or water; cover and cook on high for 9-13 minutes, stirring halfway through, until crisp-tender. Remove and let stand for 2 additional minutes.

• PEAS •

Most of us don't have the time or inclination to shell fresh peas, so the recipes below use frozen. The exception is snow peas – fresh is ideal, frozen a close second. Green peas may be flavored with butter, kosher salt and pepper. Some choose to sprinkle cooked peas with a little sugar. Spearmint, sage, or thyme adds a nice finishing touch.

• SPINACH •

Spinach is very nutritious, especially when served raw or steamed. It is a rich source of vitamin A, vitamin C, vitamin E, vitamin K, magnesium, and several vital antioxidants. As with most vegetables, fresh and frozen are best. (Sorry, Popeye, canned spinach just doesn't cut it).

To Prepare: Wash thoroughly and dry. Spinach leaves can be left whole, cut into strips, or chopped.

To Boil: Bring 8 cups of water to a boil. Add 10 ounces of spinach and cook until just wilted, about 1 or 2 minutes.

To Steam: Place 10 ounces of spinach in a steamer basket over an inch or two of boiling water. Cover and steam for 3-4 minutes, turning once.

To Microwave: Place 10 ounces of spinach in a microwave baking dish. Add 2 tablespoon chicken stock, wine, or water; cover and cook on high for 5-7 minutes, stirring halfway through, until tender. Remove and let stand for 3 additional minutes.

• YELLOW SQUASH OR ZUCCHINI •

When shopping for yellow squash or zucchini, select the smallest, heaviest and firmest squash available.

To Boil: In a saucepan, bring 6 cups of water to a boil and add 2-1/2 teaspoons kosher salt. Add 1/2 pound sliced or diced squash and return to a boil. Cook uncovered until crisp-tender, about 2 – 4 minutes until crisp-tender.

To Steam: Place 1/2 pound sliced or diced squash in a steamer basket over an inch or two of boiling water. Cover and steam for 5-7 minutes until crisp-tender.

To Microwave: Place 1/2 pound sliced or diced squash in a microwave baking dish. Add 2 tablespoon chicken stock, wine, or water; cover and cook on high for 2-4 minutes, stirring halfway through, until crisp-tender. Remove and let stand for 2 additional minutes.
Summer squash and zucchini are best served with melted butter and a sprinkling of oregano, parsley, basil, marjoram, dill, or rosemary.

• CUBAN BLACK BEANS •

When I lived in Tampa Bay and South Florida, I grew to love this dish in all of its incarnations. It seemed that every neighborhood joint had its own official Cuban recipe. Maybe someday I'll write a book detailing all of the delicious variations. Until then, I offer you this simple Table for Two recipe. I often add a 1/4 cup of chopped smoked ham to give this a little more body.

PREP: 5 minutes   COOK: 25 minutes

INGREDIENTS
    2 tablespoons olive oil
    1 small onion, chopped
    1/2 large green bell pepper, diced
    4 large garlic cloves, chopped
    1 small bay leaf
    1-1/2 teaspoons dried oregano
    1-1/2 teaspoons cumin
    1 (16-ounce) can black beans, rinsed, drained
    1/2 cup beef or vegetable broth
    1 tablespoons cider vinegar
    1/2 teaspoon sugar

DIRECTIONS
1.   Heat oil in heavy medium saucepan over medium-high heat. Add onion and bell pepper and sauté until onion turns soft and translucent, about 8 minutes. Add garlic, bay leaf, oregano, and cumin and sauté 1 additional minute.

2.   Add 1/2 cup of beans to pan and mash beans coarsely (using the back of fork). Add remaining beans and the broth. Simmer until mixture thickens and flavors blend, stirring occasionally, about 15 minutes. Stir in sugar and vinegar and cook for 3 more minutes. Season with salt and pepper to taste.

Hint: For a complete meal, add a 1/2 can of chopped tomatoes in step two and serve over steamed white rice with a fresh green salad.

• BROCCOLI WITH LEMON ALMOND BUTTER •

PREP: 5 minutes   COOK: 10 minutes

INGREDIENTS
  1/2 pound broccoli cut into bite-size pieces
  2 tablespoons unsalted butter, melted
  1 tablespoon lemon juice
  1/2 teaspoon lemon zest
  2 tablespoons blanched slivered almonds

DIRECTIONS

Steam or boil broccoli until crisp- tender, approximately 4 to 8 minutes.
Meanwhile, melt butter in a small saucepan over medium low heat. Stir in
lemon juice, lemon zest, and almonds. Pour over hot broccoli, and serve.

• BROCCOLI WITH GARLIC BUTTER •

PREP: 5 minutes   COOK: 10 minutes

INGREDIENTS
  1/2 pound fresh broccoli, cut into bite size pieces
  2 tablespoons unsalted butter
  1 teaspoon brown sugar
  1 tablespoon soy sauce
  3/4 teaspoon white vinegar
  1/8 teaspoon ground black pepper
  1 clove garlic, minced
  2 tablespoons chopped salted cashews

DIRECTIONS

Steam or boil broccoli until crisp-tender, approximately 4 to 8 minutes.
Meanwhile, melt the butter in a small skillet over medium heat. Stir in the
brown sugar, soy sauce, vinegar, pepper and garlic and bring to a boil. Stir
in the cashews to heat then pour the sauce over the broccoli to serve.

• SAUTÉED BROCCOLI WITH LEMON-PEPPER •

PREP: 5 minutes   COOK: 5 minutes

INGREDIENTS
   1-1/2 cups fresh broccoli florets
   2 tablespoons unsalted butter
   3/4 teaspoon lemon-pepper seasoning

DIRECTIONS

   Sauté broccoli in butter and lemon pepper in a 10-inch skillet over
   medium-high heat until crisp-tender, about 3-5 minutes.

• SAUTÉED BROCCOLI WITH GARLIC AND RED PEPPER •

PREP: 5 minutes   COOK: 10 minutes

INGREDIENTS
   1/2 pound broccoli, cut into bite sized pieces
   1-1/2 tablespoons extra-virgin olive oil
   1 clove garlic, minced
   Pinch red pepper flakes to taste
   Salt and pepper to taste
   Grated Parmesan cheese

DIRECTIONS

   Steam or boil broccoli until barely tender, about 4 minutes. Heat olive oil in
   a 10-inch skillet over medium-high heat. Add garlic and red pepper flakes
   and sauté for 1 or 2 minutes until their aroma is released. Add broccoli
   and sauté until crisp-tender, about 3-4 minutes. Season with salt and
   pepper to taste. Sprinkle with freshly grated Parmesan cheese.

• BROCCOLI AMANDINE •

PREP: 5 minutes   COOK: 10 minutes

INGREDIENTS
  1/2 pound broccoli stalks
  2 tablespoons unsalted butter
  1 teaspoon lemon juice or more to taste
  1 tablespoon coarsely chopped toasted almonds
  Salt and pepper to taste

DIRECTIONS

Steam or boil broccoli until crisp-tender, about 6-10 minutes. Meanwhile, in a small saucepan, melt butter and add lemon juice and almonds. Pour over broccoli and season with salt and pepper to taste.

• BROCCOLI WITH MUSTARD BUTTER AND CAPERS •

PREP: 5 minutes   COOK: 10 minutes

INGREDIENTS
  1/2 pound broccoli, cut in bite-sized pieces
  4 tablespoons unsalted butter, melted
  1 garlic clove, crushed
  1-1/2 teaspoons Dijon mustard
  1 tablespoon minced scallion
  1 tablespoon capers
  1 tablespoon chopped fresh parsley

DIRECTIONS

Steam or boil broccoli until crisp-tender, about 6-10 minutes. Melt the butter in a small saucepan over medium heat and add garlic. Cook for 1 minute and stir in mustard, scallion and parsley. Cook for 1 minute and stir in mustard, scallion, capers and parsley. Heat through and pour over broccoli.

• BROCCOLI AU GRATIN •

PREP: 10 minutes   COOK: 50 minutes

INGREDIENTS
- 1/2 pound broccoli stalks
- 3 tablespoon dried breadcrumbs, divided
- 1 tablespoon unsalted butter

For Sauce:
- 2/3 cup milk
- Small wedge onion
- Pinch ground cloves
- 1 small bay leaf
- Pinch ground nutmeg
- 1 tablespoon unsalted butter
- 1 tablespoon flour
- 3 tablespoons grated cheddar cheese

DIRECTIONS

1. Preheat oven to 425°.

2. Steam or boil broccoli until crisp-tender, about 6-10 minutes.

3. Meanwhile, heat milk, onion, clove, bay leaf and nutmeg in a small saucepan over very low heat. Simmer gently for 15 minutes. Do not boil. Remove onion and bay leaf.

4. In another small saucepan, melt the butter over low heat and stir in the flour. Cook stirring for 3-4 minutes. Remove from heat and let cook for a bit. Stir in the warmed milk, return to stove and cook, whisking, over low heat for 8 – 10 minutes until thickened. Stir in cheese to melt.

5. Sprinkle 1 tablespoon breadcrumbs in a small baking dish. Add broccoli and pour sauce over all. Top with remaining breadcrumbs and dot with butter. Bake, uncovered, until browned and bubbly, about 20 minutes.

• CARAMELIZED BRUSSELS SPROUTS AND PISTACHIOS •

PREP: 5 minutes   COOK: 30 minutes

INGREDIENTS
   1/2 pound Brussels sprouts
   2 tablespoons unsalted butter
   1 small red onion, cut into strips
   1 tablespoon red wine vinegar, divided
   1-1/2 teaspoons white sugar
   Salt and pepper to taste
   2 tablespoons coarsely chopped pistachios or toasted almonds

DIRECTIONS
   1.   Steam Brussels sprouts as above until crisp-tender, about 8-10
        minutes.

   2.   Melt the butter in a 10-inch skillet over medium-high heat. Add the
        onions and 1-1/2 teaspoons red wine vinegar and sauté until onions
        begin to brown, about 15 minutes. Add the Brussels sprouts, sugar
        and remaining vinegar. Sauté over medium heat until the sprouts are
        lightly caramelized.

   3.   Season with salt and pepper to taste and garnish with pistachios or
        almonds.

• SIMPLE BROCCOLI AU GRATIN •

A great alternative when you don't have time to create an 'au gratin' sauce from scratch. This is also excellent with cauliflower.

PREP: 5 minutes   COOK: 40 minutes

INGREDIENTS
   1/2 pound broccoli spears (or cauliflower)
   1/3 cup sour cream
   1/3 cup shredded Cheddar cheese
   1 teaspoon unsalted butter
   1/4 cup breadcrumbs

DIRECTIONS

   Preheat oven to 350°. Lightly grease a casserole dish. Steam or boil broccoli until crisp-tender, about 6-10 minutes. Place broccoli in casserole dish; add butter and toss to melt. Gently stir in sour cream and cheese. Sprinkle breadcrumbs over broccoli and bake for 25 to 30 minutes.

• BRUSSELS SPROUTS IN GARLIC BUTTER •

PREP: 10 minutes   COOK: 20 minutes

INGREDIENTS
   1/2 pound Brussels sprouts, halved
   1-1/2 tablespoons unsalted butter
   1 clove garlic, crushed
   Salt and pepper to taste
   Grated Parmesan cheese

DIRECTIONS

   Melt butter in a 10-inch skillet over medium heat. Add garlic and sauté for 1 or 2 minutes. Remove garlic with a slotted spoon Add Brussels sprouts, cut side down. Reduce heat to low, cover and cook until sprouts are tender, about 15-20 minutes. Arrange on a serving plate and sprinkle with grated Parmesan cheese.

• SIMPLE BRAISED CARROTS •

This recipe may be used as a base for a number of other carrot recipes. You may use water or to braise the carrots, but I recommend chicken broth if you're serving chicken, pork or fish, and beef broth if you are serving beef.

PREP: 5 minutes   COOK: 20 minutes

INGREDIENTS
  1/2 pound carrots, peeled and quartered lengthwise, and cut into
      2-inch lengths
  1/4 cup chicken broth, beef broth, or water
  1 tablespoon unsalted butter
  1/2 teaspoon brown sugar
  1/4 teaspoon kosher salt

DIRECTIONS

  In a medium sauté pan or skillet, add the above ingredients, cover and simmer over medium heat until carrots are tender and stock has been absorbed, about 15 – 20 minutes. When the liquid is absorbed, continue to cook carrots, stirring for an additional 3 minutes to lightly brown. Season with 1-1/2 teaspoons of your choice of chopped fresh parsley, chervil, marjoram, tarragon, or thyme and black pepper to taste.

• GLAZED CARROTS •

PREP: 5 minutes COOK: 30 minutes

INGREDIENTS
  1/2 pound carrots, braised   Salt and pepper to taste
  1 tablespoon unsalted butter   Chopped fresh parsley to
  2 tablespoons packed brown sugar   garnish

DIRECTIONS

  Braise carrots as instructed above. Reduce heat to low and stir in butter, brown sugar, salt and pepper. Cook until a syrupy glaze forms. Stir carrots to coat and sprinkle with chopped parsley.

• ORANGE GLAZED CARROTS •

PREP: 5 minutes   COOK: 30 minutes

INGREDIENTS
   1/2 pound carrots, braised
   1-1/2 tablespoons orange juice
   2-1/2 teaspoons brown sugar
   2 tablespoons unsalted butter
   3 whole cloves
   Salt to taste
   Chopped fresh parsley to garnish

DIRECTIONS

   Braise carrots as instructed above. Meanwhile, in a small saucepan, combine the orange juice, brown sugar, butter, cloves, and salt over medium heat and cook until butter melts. Pour mixture over carrots and stir to coat. Sprinkle with parsley to garnish.

• MAPLE GLAZED CARROTS •

INGREDIENTS
   1/2 pound carrots, braised
   1/4 teaspoon ground nutmeg
   1/3 cup orange juice
   1-1/2 teaspoons cornstarch
   1 -1/2 tablespoons maple syrup
   1/8 teaspoon kosher salt or more to taste
   1-1/2 tablespoons unsalted butter, melted
   1 teaspoon grated orange peel

DIRECTIONS

   Braise carrots as instructed above. Meanwhile, in a small saucepan, combine cornstarch and orange juice and stir until smooth. Add the remaining ingredients and bring to a boil. Stir for 2 minutes or until thickened. Pour glaze over carrots and gently stir to coat.

• CREAMED CARROTS •

PREP: 5 minutes   COOK: 30 minutes

INGREDIENTS
    1/2 pound carrots, braised
    1/4 cup light cream
    Herb of choice

DIRECTIONS

Braise carrots as above then add cream. Cook briefly and stir carrots to coat. Sprinkle with parsley, chervil, tarragon, chives or nutmeg.

• BABY CARROTS IN DILL •

PREP: 5 minutes   COOK: 10 minutes

INGREDIENTS
    1/2 pound baby carrots
    2 tablespoons dry white wine or chicken broth
    1 tablespoon butter
    1 teaspoon light brown sugar
    1-1/2 teaspoons chopped fresh dill (or 3/4 teaspoon dried)
    1-1/2 teaspoons fresh lemon juice
    1/8 teaspoon kosher salt
    1/8 teaspoon black pepper

DIRECTIONS

In a medium-sized heavy saucepan, combine carrots, wine, butter, sugar, salt, and dill seed. Bring to a boil; reduce heat, cover and simmer 25 to 30 minutes, or until carrots are tender and most of the liquid is absorbed. Drizzle with lemon juice and season with salt and pepper.

• CARROTS IN VERMOUTH •

PREP: 5 minutes   COOK: 15 minutes

INGREDIENTS:
  1/2 pound carrots, sliced thin or julienned
  2 teaspoons unsalted butter
  1 tablespoon sweet vermouth
  Salt and pepper to taste
  Chopped fresh parsley to garnish

DIRECTIONS

Melt butter in a 10-inch skillet over medium-high heat. Add carrots and
sauté until they just begin to brown. Add vermouth, turn heat to medium-
low and simmer for 5 more minutes, stirring often. Sprinkle with parsley to
garnish.

• CAULIFLOWER POLONAISE •

PREP: 5 minutes   COOK: 10 minutes

INGREDIENTS
  1/2 pound cauliflower florets
  1 to 2 tablespoons unsalted butter
  1/4 cup seasoned breadcrumbs
  1 tablespoon chopped hard boiled egg
  Chopped fresh parsley to garnish

DIRECTIONS

Steam or boil cauliflower as above until crisp-tender, about 3 – 8 minutes.
Place cauliflower in a serving dish and add butter. Gently stir to melt and
coat. Sprinkle with breadcrumbs and chopped egg. Garnish with parsley.

• CAULIFLOWER WITH PARSLEY AND GARLIC •

PREP: 5 minutes   COOK: 10 minutes

INGREDIENTS
    1/2 pound cauliflower florets
    1 to 2 tablespoons unsalted butter
    1 clove garlic minced
    1 to 2 tablespoons chopped fresh parsley

DIRECTIONS

Steam cauliflower as above, about 3 to 8 minutes until crisp tender. Meanwhile, melt butter in a small skillet over medium-high heat and add garlic. Sauté for 1 minute. Place cauliflower in a serving dish and pour garlic-butter over. Sprinkle with parsley and toss.

• ROASTED GARLIC CAULIFLOWER •

PREP: 10 minutes   COOK: 25 minutes

INGREDIENTS
    4 cloves garlic, minced
    1 tablespoon olive oil
    1/2 pound cauliflower florets
    2 tablespoon freshly grated Parmesan cheese
    Salt and black pepper to taste
    1 teaspoon chopped fresh parsley to garnish

DIRECTIONS

Preheat oven to 450°. Lightly grease a casserole dish. Place the olive oil and garlic in a medium bowl, add cauliflower, and toss to coat. Pour into the prepared casserole dish. Season with salt and pepper to taste. Bake for 25 minutes, stirring halfway through. Sprinkle with Parmesan cheese and parsley, and broil for 3 to 5 minutes, until golden brown.

• GREEN BEANS NIÇOISE •

PREP: 10 minutes   COOK: 45 minutes

INGREDIENTS
    2 tablespoons olive oil
    1/2 onion, sliced thin
    1/4 cup chopped celery
    1/4 cup chopped green pepper
    1 clove garlic, crushed
    1 cup canned diced tomatoes with their juice
    1 tablespoon pine nuts
    2 teaspoons lemon juice
    1 teaspoon chopped fresh chives
    1 small bay leaf
    Salt and pepper, to taste
    1/2 pound fresh green beans, cut into 1-inch lengths

DIRECTIONS
1. Heat oil in a medium saucepan over medium heat. Add onion, celery, and green pepper and sauté until onion is soft and translucent, about 10 minutes. Add garlic and sauté until fragrant, about 2 minutes.

2. Mix in tomatoes, lemon juice and pine nuts, then season with chives, bay leaf, salt and pepper. Bring to a boil, stirring often. Reduce heat and simmer gently uncovered for 25 to 30 minutes. Remove and discard bay leaf before serving.

3. Add green beans and cook until beans are crisp-tender, about 5 minutes.

• GREEN BEANS AMANDINE •

PREP: 5 minutes   COOK: 20 minutes

INGREDIENTS
  1/2 pound green beans, halved   1 tablespoon unsalted butter
  1/4 cup slivered almonds   1/2 teaspoon lemon juice
  Salt and pepper to taste

DIRECTIONS

Steam green beans until crisp-tender, about 10 – 15 minutes. Meanwhile, melt butter in a 10-inch skillet over low heat and add almonds. Cook and stir almonds until light brown and toasted. Stir in lemon juice and heat. Place green beans in a serving bowl and pour butter-almond sauce over all. Season with salt and pepper then toss to coat.

• SESAME GREEN BEANS •

PREP: 5 minutes   COOK: 25 minutes

INGREDIENTS
  1-1/2 teaspoons olive oil
  1-1/2 teaspoons sesame seeds
  1 clove garlic, crushed
  1/2 pound fresh green beans, cut into 2 inch pieces
  3 tablespoons chicken broth or dry white wine
  1/8 teaspoon kosher salt
  Freshly ground black pepper to taste

DIRECTIONS

Heat oil in a 10-inch skillet over medium heat. Add sesame seeds and sauté until seeds start to brown. Add garlic and sauté 1 additional minute. Stir in green beans. Cook, stirring, until the beans turn bright green. Add chicken broth or wine, salt and pepper. Cover and cook until beans are tender-crisp, about 10 minutes. Uncover and cook until liquid evaporates.

• GREEN BEANS WITH WATER CHESTNUTS •

PREP: 5 minutes   COOK: 15 minutes

INGREDIENTS

1/2 pound green beans, French style
1/2 cup water chestnuts, chopped
Salt and pepper to taste

1-1/2 tablespoons unsalted
 butter
1/8 teaspoon oregano

DIRECTIONS

Steam green beans until crisp tender, about 5-7 minutes. Melt butter in
a small skillet over medium-high heat. Add water chestnuts and oregano
and sauté for 3 minutes. Place green beans in a serving dish and add
water chestnuts and salt and pepper to taste. Toss to coat.

• STEAMED GREEN BEANS AND WALNUTS •

PREP: 10 minutes   COOK: 15 minutes

INGREDIENTS

1/4 cup chopped walnuts
1/2 pound green beans, trimmed and cut into 1-inch pieces
1 tablespoon unsalted butter, melted
1/2 lemon, juiced and zested
1/4 teaspoon thyme
Salt and pepper to taste

DIRECTIONS

1. Preheat oven to 375°. Arrange nuts in a single layer on a
    baking sheet. Toast in the preheated oven until lightly browned,
    approximately 5 to 10 minutes (or toast in a dry skillet until nicely
    brown).

2. Meanwhile, steam green beans as above, until crisp-tender, about
    8-10 minutes.

3. Melt butter in a 10-inch skillet over medium-high heat. Add lemon
    juice, lemon zest, and thyme. Sauté until lemon juice is nearly
    evaporated.

4. Place cooked beans in a bowl, and pour lemon butter sauce over all.

Season with salt and pepper and toss. Sprinkle with toasted walnuts.

• LEMON PEPPER PEAS •

PREP: 1 minute   COOK: 4 minutes

INGREDIENTS
   1/2 (10-ounce) package frozen green peas, thawed
   1-1/2 teaspoons water, chicken stock or dry white wine
   1 tablespoon unsalted butter
   Pinch lemon pepper
   Pinch dried dill weed

DIRECTIONS

   Place the peas and water, stock or wine into a microwave-safe bowl.
   Cover loosely, and microwave for 3 to 4 minutes, or until peas are tender.
   Stir in butter, and sprinkle with lemon pepper and dill. Serve warm.

• PEAS AND PEARL ONIONS •

PREP: 5 minutes   COOK: 5 minutes

INGREDIENTS
   1 tablespoon unsalted butter
   1 tablespoon chicken stock or dry white wine
   1/2 cup frozen pearl onions
   1/2 (10-ounce) package frozen green peas, thawed
   3 tablespoons chicken stock
   1/2 teaspoon basil
   Salt and pepper to taste

DIRECTIONS

   Melt butter in a 10-inch skillet over medium heat. Add chicken stock
   or wine and pearl onions and sauté until onions are soft, about 5 minutes.
   Add remaining ingredients and sauté until peas are tender, about
   3-5 minutes.

• PEAS AND SAUTÉED MUSHROOMS •

PREP: 10 minutes   COOK: 10 minutes

INGREDIENTS
    1/2 (10-ounce) package frozen green peas, thawed
    1-1/2 teaspoons water, chicken stock or dry white wine
    1/2 small onion, chopped
    1 clove garlic, minced
    1 tablespoon unsalted butter
    4 or 5 mushrooms, sliced
    1/2 teaspoon white sugar
    1/4 teaspoon kosher salt
    1/8 teaspoon dried thyme
    Pinch black pepper

DIRECTIONS

1. Place the peas and water, stock or wine into a microwave-safe
    bowl. Cover loosely, and microwave for 3 to 4 minutes, or until peas
    are tender.

2. Meanwhile, melt butter in a 10-inch skillet over medium heat. Sauté
    onion in butter until tender, about 5 minutes. Add garlic and sauté an
    additional minute. Stir in the peas and mushrooms and then season
    with sugar, salt, thyme and pepper. Reduce heat to low, and cook
    until heated through.

• STIR FRIED SNOW PEAS •

PREP: 5 minutes   COOK: 5 minutes

INGREDIENTS
    1/2 pound snow peas   1-1/2 teaspoon olive oil
    1-1/2 teaspoons grated ginger   1 teaspoon basil
    1/4 teaspoon kosher salt

DIRECTIONS

Remove stems and strings from snow peas if fresh. Thaw if frozen. Heat
olive oil in a 10-inch skillet over medium-high heat. Add ginger and sauté
for 30 seconds. Add peas and sauté until coated with oil and ginger.
Sprinkle with basil and salt and sauté until crisp-tender, about 3 minutes.

• CREAMED PEAS WITH MUSHROOMS •

PREP: 10 minutes   COOK: 15 minutes

INGREDIENTS
   1/2 (10-ounce) package frozen green peas, thawed
   1-1/2 teaspoons water, chicken stock or dry white wine
   1 tablespoon unsalted butter
   1/2 cup sliced fresh mushrooms
   1/2 small chopped onion
   1-1/2 teaspoons all-purpose flour
   1/2 cup light cream
   1/8 teaspoon kosher salt
   1/8 teaspoon ground black pepper
   Pinch ground nutmeg

DIRECTIONS
   1. Place the peas and water, stock or wine into a microwave-safe bowl.
       Cover loosely, and microwave for 3 to 4 minutes, or until peas are
       tender.

   2. Meanwhile, melt butter in a medium saucepan over medium heat.
       Add mushrooms and onions. Sauté for a few minutes until tender.
       Sprinkle flour over the mushrooms, and cook for 1 minute, stirring
       constantly. Gradually stir in cream then season with salt, pepper, and
       nutmeg. Cook, stirring, until smooth and thick.

   Stir in peas, and remove from heat. Let stand for 5 minutes before serving.

• SAUTÉED SPINACH AND GARLIC •

PREP: 5 minutes   COOK: 8 minutes

INGREDIENTS
 1 tablespoon extra virgin olive oil
 2 garlic cloves, minced
 1 (10-ounce) bag baby spinach leaves
 Salt and pepper to taste

DIRECTIONS

Heat olive oil in a 10-inch skillet over medium heat. Stir in garlic and sauté for one minute. Add spinach and sprinkle with salt and pepper. Sauté for 3 to 5 minutes until leaves are wilted and reduced.

• CREAMED SPINACH •

PREP: 10 minutes   COOK: 20 minutes

INGREDIENTS
 2 tablespoons unsalted butter, divided
 1/2 medium onion, chopped
 1 (10-ounce) package frozen chopped spinach, thawed and squeezed dry
 2 clove garlic, crushed
 1 tablespoon all-purpose flour
 1/2 teaspoon kosher salt
 1/4 teaspoon ground black pepper
 1/2 cup milk

DIRECTIONS

1. Melt 1 tablespoon of butter in a 10-inch skillet over medium heat. Add the onion and sauté until soft and translucent, about 10 minutes. Add the spinach and sauté until most of the liquid has evaporated.

2. In a separate small saucepan, melt the remaining butter over medium heat. Add garlic and sauté for 1 minute. Sprinkle the flour over the butter and whisk until smooth. Season with salt and pepper; cook and stir until thick. Gradually stir in the milk so that no lumps form. Simmer until thickened.

3. Add the spinach mixture to the cream sauce and mix until coated.

• QUICK SPINACH SOUFFLÉ •

PREP: 5 minutes   COOK: 20 minutes

INGREDIENTS
  1 egg, beaten plus one egg white
  1/4 cup milk
  1/4 cup grated Parmesan or Mozzarella cheese
  1 small clove garlic, crushed
  Salt and pepper to taste
  1 (10-ounce) package frozen chopped spinach, thawed and drained

DIRECTIONS

  Preheat oven to 350°. In a medium bowl whisk together egg, milk,
  cheese, garlic, salt and pepper. Fold in spinach. Place in a small casserole
  dish. Bake for 30-40 minutes, or until lightly set.

• SAUTÉED SUMMER SQUASH •

PREP: 5 minutes   COOK: 10 minutes

INGREDIENTS
  1-1/2 tablespoons olive oil
  1 clove garlic, minced
  3/4 pound yellow squash or zucchini, sliced into 1/2 inch rounds
  1-1/2 tablespoons chopped fresh parsley
  1/2 teaspoon lemon zest
  Salt and pepper to taste

DIRECTIONS

  Heat olive oil in a 10-inch skillet over medium-high heat. Add garlic and
  sauté for 1 minute. Add squash and sauté until golden and tender, about
  7 minutes. Remove to a serving bowl and toss with parsley, lemon zest,
  salt and pepper.

• STEAMED SQUASH AND SUN-DRIED TOMATOES •

PREP: 15 minutes   COOK: 15 minutes

INGREDIENTS
   3 dehydrated sun-dried tomatoes
   1 cup boiling water
   2 small zucchini, sliced
   2 small yellow squash, sliced
   1/2 sweet onion, chopped
   1 tablespoon unsalted butter
   1/4 teaspoon white sugar
   1 clove garlic, crushed
   1/8 teaspoon black pepper
   Salt to taste

DIRECTIONS
   1.   Re-hydrate tomatoes in hot water until soft, about 10 minutes.
        Remove tomatoes with a slotted spoon and coarsely chop. Reserve
        the water.

   2.   Transfer the reserved sun-dried tomato water to a saucepan and
        bring to a boil. Place the chopped sun-dried tomatoes, zucchini,
        squash, and onion in a steamer basket, and set over the boiling
        water. Reduce heat to low, cover, and simmer 15 minutes, or until
        vegetables are tender. Discard water.

   3.   Transfer the steamed vegetables to a bowl and stir in the butter,
        sugar, pepper, and salt.

• SAUTÉED SUMMER SQUASH AND TOMATOES •

PREP: 5 minutes   COOK: 30 minutes

INGREDIENTS

1 tablespoon olive oil

1 clove garlic, crushed

1 cup sliced yellow squash

1 bay leaf

1/2 teaspoon kosher salt

1/2 small onion, sliced

1 cup sliced small zucchini

1 medium tomato, chopped

1/4 teaspoon basil

1/8 teaspoon pepper

DIRECTIONS

Heat olive oil in a 10-inch skillet over medium-high heat. Add onion and sauté until soft and translucent, about 8 minutes. Add the garlic and sauté 1 additional minute. Add the zucchini, yellow squash, tomato, bay leaf, and basil. Sauté 7 minutes or until vegetables are tender. Season with salt and pepper.

• GRILLED TOMATOES WITH GARLIC AND ROSEMARY •

PREP: 5 minutes   COOK: Under 5 minutes

INGREDIENTS

1 large ripe red tomato

1 teaspoon rosemary

2 tablespoons extra virgin olive oil

2 cloves garlic, slivered

Salt and pepper to taste

DIRECTIONS

1. Preheat broiler to high.

2. Cut the tomato in half and arrange halves cut side up on a small greased baking dish. Stud the surface with garlic and rosemary then sprinkle with salt and pepper to taste. Spoon the olive oil over the tomato.

3. Place the tomatoes under the broiler and cook until the surface begins to blister and bubble. Remove from the oven (discard the garlic and rosemary if you choose) and serve.

• SAUTÉED GLAZED TOMATOES •

PREP: 10 minutes   COOK: 10 minutes

INGREDIENTS
 2 medium ripe, firm tomatoes
 1 tablespoon unsalted butter
 1-1/2 teaspoons balsamic vinegar
 1 small clove garlic, chopped
 Salt and pepper to taste

DIRECTIONS

Core the tomatoes then cut into 1-1/2 inch wedges. Heat the butter in a medium skillet over medium-high heat until butter foams. Turn the heat to high and add the tomato wedges. Sauté and turn until their color begins to dull, about 3 minutes. Add the vinegar and garlic and shake the pan until the sauce is reduced and thickened. Season with salt and pepper to taste.

• HERB BAKED TOMATOES •

PREP: 15 minutes   COOK: 20 minutes

INGREDIENTS
 2 medium ripe, firm tomatoes
 Salt and freshly ground pepper to taste
 Extra virgin olive oil
 1 tablespoon chopped fresh basil or 1 teaspoon dried oregano (or a
   combination of both)

DIRECTIONS

Preheat oven to 375°. Cut the tomatoes in half and arrange halves cut side up on a small greased baking dish. Sprinkle with salt, drizzle with olive oil, sprinkle with herbs and season with pepper. Bake until heated through and the top begins to brown, about 20 minutes.

• ROASTED RED POTATOES WITH PARMESAN •

PREP: 10 minutes   COOK: 30 minutes

INGREDIENTS

3/4 pound small whole red potatoes (halved if medium)
2 teaspoons extra virgin olive oil
2 cloves garlic, minced
1/2 teaspoon rosemary
1/4 teaspoon sage
1 teaspoon lemon zest
Salt and pepper to taste
2 tablespoons grated Parmesan cheese

DIRECTIONS

1. Preheat oven to 400°. Bring a large saucepan of water to a boil.

2. Peel a thin band around the middle of each potato with a vegetable peeler. Add potatoes to the boiling water and cook for 5 minutes. Drain.

3. Meanwhile, combine the olive oil, garlic, rosemary, and sage in a small roasting pan. Bake until garlic is fragrant, about 3-4 minutes. Add potatoes, lemon zest, salt, and pepper and toss to coat. Roast for 20 minutes, stirring occasionally, until potatoes are crisp and tender.

4. Sprinkle with Parmesan cheese and bake until cheese is melted and golden brown, about 2 minutes.

• MASHED POTATOES•

PREP: 15 minutes   COOK: 20 minutes

INGREDIENTS
2 medium russet potatoes, peeled and cubed (about 1 pound)
1/3 cup warm milk (or buttermilk)
1-1/2 tablespoons unsalted butter
1/4 teaspoon kosher salt
Pinch white pepper to taste

DIRECTIONS

Place potatoes in a saucepan and cover with water. Cover and bring to a boil; cook for 15 minutes or until very tender. Drain well. Add milk, butter, salt and pepper; mash until light and fluffy.

• GARLIC SMASHED POTATOES •

PREP: 15 minutes   COOK: 45 minutes

INGREDIENTS
1 pound unpeeled red potatoes, quartered
2 tablespoons unsalted butter
1/4 cup milk or cream, warmed
1 tablespoon grated Parmesan or Romano cheese
1 tablespoon chopped garlic
1/2 teaspoon kosher salt
1/2 teaspoon dried oregano
Pinch white pepper to taste

DIRECTIONS

Bring a large pot of salted water to a boil. Add potatoes and cook until tender but still firm, about 30 minutes; drain. Stir in butter, milk or cream, cheese, garlic, salt and oregano. Smash coarsely with a potato masher or with the back of a fork.

• DUTCH POTATOES •

PREP: 10 minutes   COOK: 15 minutes

INGREDIENTS

1/4 cup chopped onion   2 teaspoons unsalted butter
2 cups peeled, cubed potatoes   1 cup sliced fresh carrots
1/4 cup sour cream   1/4 teaspoon kosher salt
Snipped fresh chives to garnish

DIRECTIONS

1. Melt butter in a 10-inch skillet over medium-high heat. Add onions
    and sauté until soft and translucent, about 8 minutes.

2. Meanwhile, place potatoes and carrots in a large saucepan and cover
    with water. Bring to a boil. Reduce heat; cover and cook for 10-15
    minutes or until tender. Drain.

3. Mash potatoes and carrots in a small mixing bowl. Beat in onion, sour
    cream and salt. Sprinkle with chives.

• BOILED NEW POTATOES •

PREP: 5 minutes   COOK: 30 to 40 minutes

INGREDIENTS

1 pound red potatoes, the smaller the better
2 tablespoons unsalted butter
Salt and pepper to taste
Chopped fresh parsley to garnish

DIRECTIONS

1. Place potatoes in a pot with water to cover. Bring to a boil and reduce
    heat to medium. Cook at a gentle boil until potatoes are tender, 20-40
    minutes depending on size.

2. Drain potatoes and return to pot. Reduce heat to low and stir in
    butter and salt and pepper. Toss to coat.

• BASIC BAKED POTATOES •

Preheat oven to 400°. Wash and dry potatoes and pierce with a fork or knife. Bake for 45-60 minutes or until you can easily poke a hole in them. Season with salt and pepper and serve with your choice of topping: butter, sour cream, chives, cheese, etc.

• SAUTÉED NEW POTATOES WITH ROSEMARY •

PREP: 5 minutes   COOK: 30 minutes

INGREDIENTS
 1 pound medium red potatoes, cubed
 2 tablespoons olive oil
 1/4 teaspoons rosemary
 1 clove garlic, minced
 Salt and pepper to taste

DIRECTIONS

1. Place the potatoes in a pot of water and bring to a boil. Lower heat and simmer until nearly tender, 10 or 15 minutes. Drain.

2. Heat olive oil in a 10-inch skillet over medium-high heat. Add potatoes and sauté until nicely browned, about 10-20 minutes. Add rosemary and garlic and sauté for 5 additional minutes. Season with salt and pepper to taste.

• OVEN FRIES •

PREP: 10 minutes   COOK: 30 minutes

INGREDIENTS

2 large baking potatoes   1/8 teaspoon paprika
2 teaspoons olive oil   1/8 teaspoon freshly ground
1/4 teaspoon kosher salt   pepper

DIRECTIONS

1. Preheat oven to 450°.

2. Cut each potato lengthwise into eight wedges. Combine the oil, salt, paprika and pepper in a bowl. Add potato wedges and toss to coat.

3. Place in a single layer on a greased baking sheet and bake for 20 minutes. Turn potatoes and bake 10 minutes longer or until golden brown.

• SCALLOPED POTATOES WITH SOUR CREAM •

PREP: 5 minutes   COOK: 30 minutes

INGREDIENTS

2 large red or Yukon gold potatoes   1/4 teaspoon kosher salt
1/2 cup sour cream   pinch white pepper
1 egg, beaten   1/2 cup shredded sharp
1 tablespoon cream   cheddar cheese
1-1/2 tablespoons chopped fresh chives

DIRECTIONS

1. Preheat oven to 350°.

2. Cook potatoes in boiling water to cover until just tender, about 15-20 minutes. Remove and let cool. Peel and slice potatoes then arrange in a buttered baking dish.

3. Meanwhile, combine sour cream, egg, cream, chives, salt and pepper in a small bowl. Pour mixture over potatoes and sprinkle with cheese. Bake for about 30 minutes until heated through and light brown.

• STEAMED WHITE RICE •

For the life of me, I can't understand why anyone would buy instant rice. It isn't instant and it doesn't taste like rice. This recipe can be thrown together in about 20 minutes. Double or triple the amount and use the leftovers for stir-fries or a quick beans-over-rice lunch or dinner.

PREP: 5 minutes   COOK: 25 minutes

INGREDIENTS
1 tablespoon unsalted butter, divided
1/2 cup long grain rice
3/4 cup water, chicken, beef or vegetable broth
Salt and pepper to taste.

DIRECTIONS
1.   Melt half the butter in a small saucepan over medium-high heat. Add the rice and stir briefly until the grains are coated and shiny. Stir in the water or broth. Bring to a boil and cover.

2.   Lower heat and simmer for 18 minutes. Remove from heat and let stand for up to 5 minutes. Remove cover and stir in remaining butter and fluff with a fork.

Note: For extra fluffy rice, place a sturdy paper towel over the saucepan before covering with the lid. This will keep the condensation from falling back into the rice as it steams.

• RICE PILAF •

This basic rice dish goes well with just about any meal. It's quick and versatile - simply substitute beef or vegetable broth for the chicken depending on your main course. Feel free to experiment with the herbs as well: basil, oregano, marjoram, or summer savory goes well with this dish. Since this is so delicious, I usually double the recipe to serve with whatever leftovers I have in the fridge.

PREP: 5 minutes   COOK: 25 minutes

INGREDIENTS
- 1 tablespoon unsalted butter, divided
- 1 tablespoon minced onion
- 1/4 teaspoon minced garlic
- 1/2 cup long grain rice
- 3/4 cup chicken or beef broth
- 1/2 teaspoon chopped fresh parsley
- 1/8 teaspoon dried thyme
- Dash of Worcestershire sauce
- Dash of hot pepper sauce
- 1 small bay leaf

DIRECTIONS
1. Melt half the butter in a small saucepan over medium-high heat and sauté the onion and garlic until the onion soft and translucent. Add the rice and stir briefly until the grains are coated and shiny.

2. Stir in the broth and add the parsley, thyme, Worcestershire sauce, hot pepper sauce and bay leaf. Bring to a boil and cover. Lower heat and simmer for 18 minutes.

3. Remove cover and discard bay leaf. Stir in remaining butter and fluff with a fork.

• RICE WITH PINE NUTS AND RAISINS •

PREP: 5 minutes   COOK: 25 minutes

INGREDIENTS

1 tablespoon unsalted butter, divided
1 tablespoon minced onion
1/4 teaspoon minced garlic
1/2 cup long grain rice
2 tablespoons raisins
3/4 cup chicken or vegetable broth
2 tablespoons pine nuts
Salt and pepper to taste

DIRECTIONS

1. Melt half the butter in a small saucepan over medium-high heat and sauté the onion and garlic until the onion soft and translucent. Add the rice and stir briefly until the grains are coated and shiny.

2. Stir in the broth and add the raisins. Bring to a boil and cover. Lower heat and simmer for 18 minutes.

3. Remove cover and stir in remaining butter, add the pine nuts and fluff with a fork. Season with salt and pepper to taste.

• RICE AND PEAS •

PREP: 5 minutes   COOK: 25 minutes

INGREDIENTS
  1-1/2 tablespoons unsalted butter, divided
  1 tablespoon minced onion
  1/2 cup rice
  3/4 cup chicken or vegetable broth
  1 small bay leaf
  Salt and pepper to taste
  1 to 2 drops hot pepper sauce (or to taste)
  1/2 cup frozen peas
  1 tablespoon chopped fresh parsley

DIRECTIONS

1.   Melt 1 tablespoon butter in a small saucepan over medium heat. Add the onion and sauté until soft. Add rice and stir until coated and shiny.

2.   Stir in broth, bay leaf, salt, pepper and hot pepper sauce. Bring to a boil and cover. Lower heat and simmer for 18 minutes.

3.   Meanwhile, place the peas and remaining butter in a small pan and cook, shaking for about one minute until peas are cooked but firm (or place in a bowl and microwave).

4.   Add the peas and parsley to the finished rice and stir.

• RICE WITH WINE AND TOMATOES •

This full-bodied version of a pilaf is very similar to risotto, without the needed attention.

PREP: 5 minutes   COOK: 30 minutes

INGREDIENTS
  1 tablespoon olive oil
  1/2 cup chopped onion
  3/4 cup long grained rice
  Salt and pepper to taste
  1/2 cup dry white (or red) wine
  1/2 cup diced tomatoes (canned is fine)
  Grated Parmesan cheese to garnish
  1 cup chicken, beef, or vegetable broth

DIRECTIONS
  1. Heat oil in a medium saucepan over medium-high heat. Add the onion and sauté until soft and translucent, about 8 minutes.

  2. Reduce heat to medium and add the rice. Stir to coat and season well. Add the wine and cook for 2 or 3 minutes. Return the heat to medium-high and add the broth and tomatoes. Bring to a boil.

  3. Turn the heat to low and cover. Cook for 20 minutes and check to see if rice is tender and the liquid is absorbed. Sprinkle with Parmesan.

• ORANGE RICE •

PREP: 10 minutes   COOK: 30 minutes

INGREDIENTS
1/4 cup chopped onion
1/4 cup chopped green pepper
1/4 cup chopped sweet red pepper
1 teaspoon olive oil
1/2 cup uncooked long grain rice
3/4 cup chicken broth
1/4 cup orange juice
1/8 teaspoon kosher salt
Dash pepper
1/2 (11-ounce) can mandarin oranges, drained and coarsely chopped

DIRECTIONS

1. Heat olive oil in a small saucepan over medium heat. Sauté onion and peppers until tender, about 10 minutes. Add rice and stir until lightly browned.

2. Add broth, orange juice, salt and pepper. Bring to a boil then reduce heat to medium-low. Cover and simmer for 15-20 minutes or until liquid is absorbed. Stir in oranges.

• BASIC BROWN RICE •

PREP: Less than 5 minutes   COOK: 40 to 55 minutes

INGREDIENTS
   1/2 cup brown rice
   1 to 1-1/4 cups water, chicken, beef or vegetable broth
   1/4 teaspoon dried marjoram, summer savory, or thyme
   1 tablespoon minced onion
   1-1/2 teaspoons unsalted butter
   Salt and pepper to taste

DIRECTIONS

Bring the water (or broth) and butter to a boil in a small saucepan. Stir in rice, marjoram, and onion. Cover and cook over very low heat until liquid is absorbed, about 35 - 45 minutes. Remove from heat and let stand for an additional 5 or 10 minutes. Add salt and pepper to taste.

Note: If the rice is tender but still chewy and the liquid has been absorbed, add a tablespoon or so of broth and continue to simmer for a few more minutes. If after the allotted time, the rice is tender but some broth remains, remove from the heat and keep covered for 5 or 10 minutes.

• BROWN RICE WITH CASHEWS AND HERBS •

PREP: 5 minutes   COOK: 45 minutes

INGREDIENTS
  1 tablespoon olive oil
  1/2 cup chopped onion
  1 clove garlic, minced
  1/2 cup brown rice
  1/4 cup cashew pieces
  1 small bay leaf
  1/4 teaspoon dried thyme
  Salt and pepper to taste
  1 cup chicken, beef or vegetable broth
  Chopped fresh parsley to garnish

DIRECTIONS

  1.   Heat olive oil in a medium saucepan over medium heat. Add onion
       and sauté until soft and translucent, about 10 minutes. Add garlic and
       sauté an additional minute. Add brown rice and cashews and stir to
       coat well. Stir in herbs, salt, pepper, and broth.

  2.   Bring to a boil, cover and turn the heat to low. Simmer for 30 - 40
       minutes until the liquid is absorbed and the rice is tender. Remove the
       bay leaf and garnish with parsley.

See special note above regarding brown rice.

• BUTTERED NOODLES •

PREP: 5 minutes   COOK: 3 to 9 minutes

INGREDIENTS
  1/4 pound noodles of choice
  1 tablespoon unsalted butter at room temperature
  Salt and pepper to taste

DIRECTIONS

Drop the noodles into 1 quart of salted boiling water. Return to a boil and cook as directed on the noodle package. Do not overcook. Drain the noodles and toss with the butter and salt and pepper to taste.

• BUTTERED NOODLES WITH CARROTS • AND POPPY SEEDS

PREP: 5 minutes   COOK: 5 to 9 minutes

INGREDIENTS
  1 medium carrot, peeled
  1/4 pound egg noodles
  1-1/2 tablespoons unsalted butter at room temperature
  1-1/2 teaspoons poppy seeds
  Salt and pepper to taste

DIRECTIONS

1. Bring 1 cup of water to a boil in a small saucepan over medium-high heat. Cut the carrot into matchsticks (julienne) and add to the water. Simmer for about 3 minutes or until carrots are crisp tender. Drain.

2. Meanwhile, bring 1 quart of salted water to a boil and add the noodles. Cook according to the noodle package. (Do not overcook). Drain the noodles and return them to the saucepan and add the butter and carrots. Sprinkle with the poppy seeds and toss. Season with salt and pepper to taste.

• BUTTERED NOODLES WITH NUTMEG •

Prepare noodles as above adding 1/8 teaspoon nutmeg at the end. Toss and serve.

• BUTTERED NOODLES WITH DILL •

Prepare noodles as above adding 1 tablespoon fresh dill (or 1-1/2 teaspoons dried) at the end. Toss and serve.

• BUTTERED NOODLES WITH CARAWAY SEEDS •

Prepare noodles as above adding 1/4 teaspoon caraway seeds at the end. Toss and serve.

• PARMESAN NOODLES •

PREP: 5 minutes   COOK: 20 minutes

INGREDIENTS
   1/4 pound medium egg noodles
   1-1/2 tablespoons chopped green onions
   1 tablespoon unsalted butter, at room temperature
   1/4 cup grated fresh Parmesan cheese
   Garlic salt and pepper to taste

DIRECTIONS
       Cook noodles according to package directions; drain. Toss with
       onions, butter, Parmesan cheese, garlic salt, and pepper.

Desserts

 # Desserts

When many of us think of desserts, we think of cakes, pies, and ice cream. Unfortunately, it's not easy to bake a pie or cake for two. If you have the craving for cakes or pies, I encourage you to purchase one of the fine selections available from your grocer or baker. But if you really enjoy baking, by all means, whip out the recipes you love and go to town. I have several that I'd love to share with you. Unfortunately, they aren't for two (or even four) and therefore don't fit within the scope of this book.

What about homemade ice cream? It's do-able, but definitely not a quick and simple dessert for two. Why go through the trouble when you can pick up some Häagen Dazs, Ben and Jerry's or Breyers from your grocer's freezer? Besides, when was the last time you had homemade ice cream that even came close to these brands? Don't fret. I can't remember, either.

Instead, I'm offering some deliciously different, and truly Table for Two desserts. Quickly prepared and loaded with fruit, cream, and other fresh ingredients, these selections will satisfy the most discriminating sweet tooth - recipes like Pears Poached in Port, Grilled Peach Sundaes and Mixed Berry Parfaits.

• FROZEN RASPBERRY CHEESECAKE •

PREP: 5 minutes   CHILL: 4 hours

INGREDIENTS

   1/4 cup crushed shortbread cookies
   1 tablespoon unsalted butter, melted
   1-1/2 ounces cream cheese, softened
   3 tablespoons sweetened condensed milk
   1 tablespoon lemon juice
   1/3 cup raspberry sherbet, softened
   1/4 cup fresh raspberries

DIRECTIONS

Combine the cookie crumbs and butter in a small bowl then press into the bottom of two 6-ounce ramekins coated with nonstick cooking spray. In another small bowl, combine the cream cheese, milk and lemon juice until blended. Spread over crust and freeze for 2 hours or until firm. Spread sherbet over cream cheese layer and freeze for 2 more hours until firm. Top with raspberries and serve.

• MIXED BERRY PARFAIT •

PREP: 15 minutes

INGREDIENTS

   1/3 cup reduced-fat granola cereal, divided
   1 (8-ounce) carton reduced-fat vanilla yogurt
   1/2 cup fresh raspberries
   1/2 cup fresh blackberries or blueberries

DIRECTIONS

Place 2 tablespoons of granola in each of two parfait glasses. Top each with about 2 tablespoons yogurt. Combine the raspberries and blackberries; divide a third of the mixture between the two glasses. Repeat yogurt and berry layers. Top with the remaining yogurt, berries and granola.

• GRILLED PEACH SUNDAE •

Fruit on the grill? Why not? This is a great dessert when you already have the grill fired up. Try this with other stone fruit and pineapple, too!

PREP: 5 minutes   COOK: 10 minutes

INGREDIENTS
    2 peaches, halved and pitted
    1 teaspoon vegetable oil
    2 scoops vanilla ice cream
    1 tablespoon toasted unsweetened coconut

DIRECTIONS

Preheat grill to high. Brush peach halves with oil. Grill until tender. Place 2 peach halves in each bowl and top with a scoop of ice cream or frozen yogurt. Sprinkle with coconut.

• CHOCOLATE COVERED CHERRIES •

PREP: 5 minutes   COOK: 5 minutes

INGREDIENTS
    12 ounces milk chocolate, chopped
    8 ounces milk
    10 cherries with stems

DIRECTIONS

Using a double boiler, heat the chocolate until melted. Stir in milk, using enough to make the chocolate smooth. Holding the cherries by their stems, dip them one by one into the chocolate mixture. Place the coated cherries on wax paper and let sit until the chocolate has dried.

• BLUEBERRY PEAR CRISPS •

PREP: 10 minutes   COOK: 20 minutes

INGREDIENTS
1 small pear, peeled and chopped
1/2 cup fresh or frozen blueberries
2 tablespoons brown sugar
1 tablespoon all-purpose flour
1 tablespoon quick cooking oats
1/8 teaspoon ground cinnamon
1 tablespoon cold unsalted butter
Whipped cream or vanilla ice cream

DIRECTIONS

1.   Preheat oven to 350°.

2.   Divide the fruit between two 6-oz. ramekins or custard cups coated
     with nonstick cooking spray. In a bowl, combine the brown sugar,
     flour, oats and cinnamon; cut in butter until mixture is crumbly.
     Sprinkle over fruit.

3.   Bake at 350° for 20-25 minutes or until topping is golden brown. Top
     with whipped cream or vanilla ice cream and serve.

• PEARS POACHED IN PORT •

PREP: 10 minutes   COOK: 8 minutes
COOL TIME: 30 minutes

INGREDIENTS
  2 cups tawny port wine
  1/2 cup water
  1/4 cup sugar
  1/2 vanilla bean, split lengthwise and scraped, seeds and pod reserved
  1 (1-inch) stick cinnamon
  1/2 teaspoon whole allspice
  Pinch of kosher salt
  2 firm Bosc or Anjou pears

DIRECTIONS

1. Combine all ingredients except pears in a medium saucepan and bring
    to a boil over medium-high heat. Stir to dissolve sugar. Meanwhile, peel
    pears, leaving the stems intact. Slice off the bottom 1/8 inch of each
    pear to create a flat, stable base.

2. Reduce heat to low and add pears, laying them on their sides so
    that they are almost completely submerged. Simmer, turning pears
    occasionally, until they are well-saturated and barely tender when
    pierced with a fork, about 6 to 8 minutes.

3. Allow pears to cool completely in the poaching liquid. Serve or transfer
    pears and liquid to an airtight container and store in the refrigerator for
    up to 2 days.

• TOASTED-COCONUT TAPIOCA •

PREP: 5 minutes   COOK: 10 minutes

INGREDIENTS
   3/4 cup light coconut milk
   3/4 cup fat-free milk
   3 tablespoons sugar
   4 teaspoons uncooked quick-cooking tapioca
   2 tablespoons egg substitute
   Pinch of kosher salt
   1/4 teaspoon vanilla extract
   2 tablespoons flaked sweetened coconut, toasted

DIRECTIONS

   Combine the first 6 ingredients in a medium saucepan, and let stand
   5 minutes. Bring to a boil over medium-high heat, stirring constantly.
   Remove from heat, and stir in vanilla. Divide mixture evenly between 2
   dessert bowls. Cover and chill until thick. Sprinkle each serving with 1
   tablespoon toasted coconut.

• DRIED PLUMS IN BEAUJOLAIS •

PREP: 5 minutes   MARINATE: 24 hours
COOK: 30 minutes   CHILL: 1 hour

INGREDIENTS
   1 pound large pitted dried plums (prunes)
   1-1/2 cups Beaujolais wine
   1/2 teaspoon vanilla extract
   1 cup sugar
   Grated peel from one lemon

DIRECTIONS

   Combine the dried plums and the wine in a medium bowl. Let stand
   24 hours at room temperature. Transfer the dried plums and wine to a
   saucepan. Add the vanilla, sugar and lemon peel. Bring to a boil, reduce
   heat and simmer for 30 minutes until it becomes syrupy. Chill. Remove
   lemon peel and serve with vanilla ice cream.

• CHILLED MIXED FRUIT IN WHITE WINE •

PREP: 10 minutes   COOK: 2 minutes
CHILL: 2 + Hours

INGREDIENTS
   3/4 cup dry white wine
   3 tablespoons white sugar
   1-1/2 teaspoons chopped fresh mint
   1/2 cantaloupe, cut into bite-size pieces
   1/2 cup seedless green grapes, halved
   1 cup fresh strawberries, hulled and halved

DIRECTIONS

1.   Combine the wine and sugar in a medium saucepan over medium
     heat and bring to a boil; stirring to dissolve sugar. Remove the
     saucepan from the heat and add the mint; set aside.

2.   Combine the cantaloupe, grapes, and strawberries in a large bowl.
     Pour the wine mixture over the fruit; toss together until all the fruit is
     covered with the wine mixture; cover and chill. Store in the refrigerator
     up to 8 hours before serving.

Breakfast

• POACHED EGGS •

Breakfast doesn't get much easier then this.

INGREDIENTS
   4 eggs
   1 teaspoon white vinegar
   1 teaspoon kosher salt

DIRECTIONS

   Bring about 1/2 inch of water to a boil in 10-inch skillet. Add vinegar and
   salt and reduce to barely a simmer. Crack each egg into a cup or small
   bowl and gently pour into the water, careful that the eggs don't touch.
   Cook until the whites are set and the yolk has filmed over. Remove
   eggs (trim ragged edges if desired) and serve on toasted bread or
   English muffins.

• BAKED EGGS •
(OEUFS EN COCOTTE)

A simple and elegant breakfast recipe, these eggs are baked in individual
ramekins and are a great way to use leftover veggies.

INGREDIENTS
   2 or 4 eggs at room temperature
   Vegetables of choice (tomatoes, creamed spinach, sautéed mushrooms,
      leftover cooked veggies)
   2 – 4 tablespoons heavy cream
   Salt and pepper to taste
   Freshly grated Parmesan cheese

DIRECTIONS
Preheat oven to 350°. Lightly butter each ramekin. Place a tablespoon
of vegetables in the bottom then break an egg in each ramekin. Spoon a
tablespoon or two of cream over each egg, season with salt and pepper to
taste, then sprinkle with cheese. Place the ramekins in a baking dish large
enough to hold them and add enough boiling water to come up half way.
Bake until the egg white sets but the yolk is still runny. About 10 minutes.
Serve with toast wedges.

• SCRAMBLED EGGS •

The French insist on taking 45 minutes or more to make scrambled eggs. Sure the result is a luxurious treat unlike anything you've ever tasted at the neighborhood hash house, but who has that kind of time and patience? I rarely do, so here's a version that falls between the 30 second scrambled egg we've grown accustomed to and the painstakingly detailed continental version. I think you'll be happy.

INGREDIENTS
1 tablespoon unsalted butter
4 eggs (at room temperature if possible)
1 or 2 tablespoons water
Salt and pepper to taste

DIRECTIONS

Crack the eggs in a small bowl and beat until the yolks and whites are combined. Add the water and beat until incorporated. Meanwhile, heat a 10-inch skillet over medium heat for 1 minute. Add the butter and swirl. Turn the heat to medium-low and add the eggs. Stir until the eggs begin to set and have lost their runniness, about 3 or 4 minutes. Season with salt and pepper and serve immediately.

CREATIVE SCRAMBLED EGG VARIATIONS.

Add:
 3 tablespoons of diced cream cheese for a luxurious flavor
1/2 cup sautéed mushrooms
1/2 cup sautéed or leftover diced veggies
1/2 to 1 cup diced tomatoes
1/2 cup diced cooked shrimp
1/2 cup leftover chili or Cuban black beans
1/2 cup minced smoked fish (salmon, mullet, etc.)
1/2 cup prepared salsa, drained
Tabasco® or Worcestershire sauce to taste

• GREEK-STYLE FETA EGGS •
(STRAPATSATHA)

INGREDIENTS

1 tablespoon unsalted butter
1/4 cup chopped onion
4 eggs at room temperature
1 tablespoon water

1/4 cup chopped tomatoes
2 tablespoons crumbled feta
   cheese
Salt and pepper to taste

DIRECTIONS

1. Heat a 10-inch skillet over medium heat for 1 minute. Add the butter and swirl to melt. Add onions and sauté until translucent, about 8 – 10 minutes. Add tomatoes and cook for 5 additional minutes.

2. Meanwhile, crack the eggs in a small bowl and beat until the yolks and whites are combined. Add the water and beat until incorporated. Turn the heat to medium-low and add the eggs. Stir until the eggs begin to set and have lost their runniness, about 3 or 4 minutes. When eggs appear almost done, stir in the feta cheese and season with salt and pepper. Cook until cheese is melted.

• GLAZED CANADIAN BACON •

Tired of the same-old, same-old breakfast meats? Check out this recipe. I guarantee it will become a part of your breakfast rotation.

INGREDIENTS

1 tablespoon Dijon mustard
1 teaspoon pure maple syrup
Pinch of cayenne pepper to taste (a little goes a long way!)
1/2 pound Canadian bacon, 1/4-inch slice

DIRECTIONS

Preheat broiler. Whisk the mustard, syrup and cayenne in a small bowl. Place bacon on a broiler pan or baking sheet and broil 3 inches from the heat for 3 – 4 minutes. Turn and brush with the glaze. Broil for 3 – 4 minutes more or until bacon is well done.

• BREAKFAST BURRITOS •

INGREDIENTS
- 1/4 pound sliced bacon or breakfast sausage
- 1-1/2 teaspoons unsalted butter
- 1/2 medium onion, chopped
- 1/3 cup chopped green or red pepper
- 3 eggs
- 1-1/2 teaspoons water
- 1/4 teaspoon kosher salt
- 1/8 teaspoon freshly ground pepper
- 1 cup shredded sharp Cheddar cheese
- 2 (10-inch) flour tortillas, warmed
- Prepared salsa (hot, medium or mild) to taste

DIRECTIONS
1. Heat a 10-inch skillet over medium heat for 1 minute. Add the bacon or sausage until crisp (bacon) or cooked through (sausage). Remove to a small bowl and crumble.

2. Wipe skillet and return to heat. Add butter and swirl to melt. Add onion and green pepper and sauté until onions are translucent, about 8 – 10 minutes.

3. Meanwhile, crack the eggs in a small bowl and beat until the yolks and whites are combined. Add the water and beat until incorporated. Pour over vegetables in the skillet. Sprinkle with cheese and bacon. Cook and stir gently over medium heat until the eggs are completely set.

4. Spoon 1/2 of the eggs down the center of each tortilla; fold sides over filling. Serve with salsa if desired.

• TOP 'O THE MORNIN' BREAKFAST •

This one-skillet breakfast dish is the perfect way to start off a cold Saturday morning. It's also a great way to used leftover potatoes, tomatoes, or that half onion and pepper you have in the fridge.

INGREDIENTS
   1/4 pound bacon, sausage or chopped ham
   1 tablespoon unsalted butter
   3 potatoes, peeled and thinly sliced
   1/2 onion, minced
   1/2 green bell pepper, chopped
   1/2 cup chopped tomatoes (optional)
   3 eggs at room temperature

DIRECTIONS
   1. Heat a 10-inch skillet over medium heat for 1 minute. Add the bacon or sausage and cook until done. Remove to a bowl and keep warm.

   2. Pour out all but 1 tablespoon fat then raise heat to medium-high. Add butter to skillet and swirl to melt. Stir in potatoes, onion, green pepper and tomatoes (if using); sauté until potatoes are browned. Stir in eggs and bacon, sausage or ham and cook until eggs are set. Serve immediately.

Note: you can also make this with frozen hash browns or shredded potatoes. Adjust timing according to package label.

• FRITTATTAS – OMELETS FOR THE REST OF US •

We know the French perfected the omelet. We also know that a perfectly formed and cooked omelet is a sight to behold and taste at the morning breakfast table. We also know that few of us have the knack to make one correctly. Leave it up to the Italians to create an omelet that not only rewards the taste buds, but is also incredibly simple to prepare and nearly foolproof. Once you learn to make the basic frittata and some of its variations, you'll find yourself creating new and inventive frittatas for breakfast or brunch (and dinner, too!).

• BASIC FRITTATA•

INGREDIENTS

1 tablespoon unsalted butter or olive oil
3 eggs
1/4 cup freshly grated Parmesan (or other cheese)
Salt and pepper to taste

DIRECTIONS

1. Preheat oven broiler.

2. Heat a 10-inch skillet over medium heat for 1 minute. Add the butter and swirl to melt. Meanwhile, beat the eggs in a small bowl with the cheese and salt and pepper.

3. Pour the eggs into the skillet and turn heat to medium-low. Cover and cook, undisturbed, until the eggs start to set and the bottom is firm, about 10 minutes.

4. Uncover skillet and broil about 5 inches from heat for 1 – 3 minutes until the top is just set and is flecked with brown. Do not overcook.

• SPINACH MUSHROOM FRITTATA •

INGREDIENTS

2 garlic cloves, minced or crushed
1 medium onion, chopped
2 teaspoons olive oil or unsalted butter, divided
2 cups sliced mushrooms
1/4 teaspoon dried thyme
5 ounces spinach, stemmed, rinsed and dried
3 eggs
1/2 teaspoon dried dill
Salt and pepper to taste
1/4 cup grated Parmesan or crumbled feta cheese

DIRECTIONS

1. Preheat oven broiler.

2. Heat 1 teaspoon olive oil in a 10-inch skillet over medium heat. Add onions and sauté until soft and translucent, about 8 – 10 minutes. Add garlic and sauté 1 additional minute. Stir in mushrooms and thyme; continue to sauté until mushrooms begin to lose their moisture, about 5 more minutes.

3. Meanwhile, cook spinach in a saucepan over low heat with just the water that clings to it from rinsing until it just begins to wilt (if using frozen spinach, heat in microwave to defrost and squeeze well to remove water). Drain and cool, then chop.

4. In a medium bowl, beat the eggs, dill, salt and pepper until well-combined. Stir in mushrooms, spinach, and cheese. Heat remaining teaspoon olive oil to skillet over medium heat and pour in egg mixture.

5. Cover and cook, undisturbed, until the eggs start to set and the bottom is firm, about 10 minutes. Uncover skillet and broil about 5 inches from heat for 1 – 3 minutes until the top is just set and is flecked with brown. Do not overcook.

• TOMATO, GARLIC AND POTATO FRITTATA •

INGREDIENTS
   3 eggs
   1/4 cup freshly grated Parmesan cheese, divided
   2 tablespoons sliced fresh basil leaves
   1/2 teaspoon kosher salt, divided
   1/4 teaspoon freshly ground pepper
   1-1/2 tablespoons olive oil, divided
   2 cloves garlic, thinly sliced
   1/4 pound red potatoes, peeled and diced
   1 cup halved cherry tomatoes

DIRECTIONS

1. Preheat oven broiler.

2. Whisk the eggs, 2 tablespoons cheese, 1/4 teaspoon salt and pepper together in a medium bowl.

3. Heat 1/2 tablespoon olive oil in a 10-inch skillet over medium heat. Add garlic and sauté about 1 minute. Remove garlic with a slotted spoon to a small bowl.

4. Turn heat to medium-high and add potatoes to the skillet. Stir until just tender, about 5 -6 minutes. Transfer potatoes to the bowl with the garlic.

5. Add 1/2 tablespoon olive oil to skillet and add tomatoes. Sauté until tomato skins begin to brown and split, about 4 minutes.

6. Add remaining olive oil to skillet. Add potatoes and garlic and spread evenly across the skillet. Season with remaining salt and additional pepper to taste. Pour eggs over potatoes and lightly stir to incorporate. Cook for 3 minutes. Cover and cook over medium heat an additional 5 – 7 minutes until eggs begin to set. Remove cover and sprinkle with remaining cheese and broil about 5 inches from heat for 2 – 3 minutes until the top is just set and is flecked with brown. Do not overcook.

NOW, WHAT ABOUT THE LEFTOVERS?

Some of these recipes call for only 1/2 a can of chopped tomatoes, or 1/2 a package frozen vegetables. Some call for just a tablespoon of chopped fresh parsley or other herb. Perhaps you found some meat on sale and cooked up a batch. What do you do with the rest? Don't toss it. Here are some delicious and frugal ideas for your leftovers:

VEGGIES:
Soups: Bring two cups of beef, chicken, or vegetable broth to a boil and add the leftover veggies, tomatoes, and/or potatoes. Reduce heat and add 1/4 teaspoon dried thyme, oregano, basil or other herb of choice. Simmer until everything is cooked or warmed through. Salt and pepper to taste.

- Add diced cooked beef, chicken, or pork if you have it on hand and heat through.
- Add leftover beans or rice.
- Stir in a handful of pasta to the boiling broth and cook until á la denté. Then add veggies and cooked meat and heat through.

Breakfast or Brunch: Use leftover veggies to create a unique omelet, frittata, or scrambled egg dish. For something a little more elegant use left over veggies in baked eggs.

Stir Fry: Use broccoli, cauliflower, carrots, or squash to create a stir-fry.

FRESH HERBS: Chop herbs and place one tablespoon into each square of an ice cube tray. Add water to cover and freeze. Remove cubes and place in a labeled freezer bag. Add frozen cubes to soups, stews, gratins, sauces, and other dishes.

MEATS: Thinly slice beef or pork and reheat in a bit of broth to make sandwiches.

Slice leftover beef or pork into thin strips for stir-fries.

Dice leftover beef or pork and add to soups.

Heat a can of drained red or black beans in 1/2 cup broth. Add diced beef or pork, and season with oregano and chili powder to taste for a quick chili lunch. Add leftover diced tomatoes if you have them.

FISH AND SHELLFISH: Diced cooked fish and whole shrimp can be served over a bed of greens with your choice of salad dressing.

Bring a cup of fish or clam broth and cream to a simmer and add some sautéed onions and diced, cooked fish or shrimp for a quick chowder. Throw in some cubed potatoes if you have them.

Index

27459222R00150

Made in the USA
Columbia, SC
25 September 2018